MW01015242

THE VICTORIAN HOME
IN AMERICA

THE VICTORIAN HOME
IN AMERICA

With Over 250 Illustrations

John Maass

DOVER PUBLICATIONS, INC.
Mineola, New York

Copyright

Copyright © 1972 by John Maass
All rights reserved under Pan American and International Copyright Conventions.

Published in Canada by General Publishing Company, Ltd., 30 Lesmill Road, Don Mills, Toronto, Ontario.

Bibliographical Note

This Dover edition, first published in 2000, is a slightly altered reprint of the edition first published by Hawthorn Books, Inc., New York, in 1972. Thirty color plates have been omitted.

International Standard Book Number: 0-486-41252-0

Manufactured in the United States of America
Dover Publications, Inc., 31 East 2nd Street, Mineola, N.Y. 11501

To our children,
Valerie and Andrew

FOREWORD

In 1957 I published a book called *The Gingerbread Age*, subtitled *A View of Victorian America*. In a one-page foreword I expressed the hope that it would "serve as an antidote to long-entrenched clichés."

Within days of publication a torrent of fan mail began to arrive. My vanity was flattered by gracious compliments on the creamy stationery of distinguished scholars and public personages. My heart was touched by messages on ruled paper from the dime store because it was evident that they came from people who wrote few letters and bought few books. These notes said: "We love our home, but people poked fun at it. . . . Now we show them your book, and we don't have to be ashamed anymore. . . . Thank you so much for writing this book." Some readers wrote me about places I should visit, like Constantine, Michigan, or Palestine, Texas. Some sent me gifts. A lady in New England remembered me with fringed Victorian Christmas cards she had found in the attic; a gentleman in California sent me photographs of the gingerbread house he had built for his cat to live in (he made shingles from the round ends of Popsicle sticks). After fourteen years and three printings the flood of letters has diminished, but it has never ceased.

I was pleased that quotations from my text showed up in dissertations, articles, and books—with or without mention of the source. I have an excellent visual memory, and I was delighted to see that artists kept adapting my pictures to produce their paintings, drawings, illustrations, book jackets, greeting cards, ads, cartoons, and stage sets.

It seemed that everybody agreed: Victorian was wonderful. It was, of course, not my book that brought about this reversal of public opinion. The book had simply appeared at the time when a new view of Victorian arts and civilization was due. Since then Art Nouveau, Edwardian art, and Art Deco have, in turn, regained favor, but the interest in Victoriana has not faded. I conducted an aggressive defense of Victorianism in 1957; in this book I will not keep saying how great Victorian design is. There is no need. Victorian architecture is forever. It is as valid as the paintings of the Italian Renaissance, the bronzes of West Africa, or the carvings of the Kwakiutl Indians of the Northwest.

This book deals with American domestic architecture of the years 1840 to 1900, though any such "periodization" must always be arbitrary. I urge the reader to keep in mind that history is a flowing stream that does not start and stop by centuries or decades.

I have reluctantly omitted public buildings, though they have had an important influence on private houses. To include public architecture would have tripled the size of this volume. Nor have I discussed gardens, though they are closely linked with the topic of homes. Victorian garden design merits a book by a qualified author.

Private enterprise and individual ownership have been dominant in America. This may be the reason that American architectural history has been written entirely in terms of individual buildings, although Lewis Mumford pointed out long ago that "except in the abstraction of drawing or photography, no building exists in a void." Historians have failed to relate houses to community and environment. This book also falls short in this respect, but I have made a determined effort to present illustrations that show homes in their natural and man-made settings.

Two-dimensional pictures of three-dimensional architecture are inevitably inadequate. For that very reason I have worked with the utmost tenacity to provide the best possible illustrations, carefully checking more than 500,000 new and old views to select just about 250.

There is a bad tradition in architectural photography of showing houses and rooms without people, though no one has ever seen a room or a house without at least one person having been present. Roped-off "period rooms" in museums are often handsome and popular, but they are not the real thing. Somerset Maugham wrote a story in which a newly rich family pretends to be old gentry. The narrator sees through the pose because their country house is too perfect: All the furnishings are of "museum quality," and the house lacks the watercolors painted by an aunt, the souvenirs from a trip, the kind of things that accumulate in a home over the years. I have avoided lifeless stock photographs. Instead, I have searched long and hard for pictures of Victorian people in their Victorian homes to convey a sense of place and time.

If the words and images in this book help some readers to become more aware of their own environment, I will be content.

J. M.

ACKNOWLEDGMENTS

This book is based upon primary sources—Victorian records and the Victorian buildings themselves—but I have also drawn freely on the knowledge of my contemporaries. I have consulted hundreds of persons and organizations throughout America, so that it would not be practicable to list them all here. I will single out only a few who helped far beyond the call of their regular duties:

I have learned much from the writings and conversation of Alan Gowans, a scholar of Victorian civilization who is, appropriately, at the University of Victoria.

I am indebted to the Historic American Buildings Survey, its former director, James C. Massey, and its chief historian, Denys Peter Myers.

The approach of this book also owes something to two books by distinguished European scholars: James Laver's *Style in Costume* and Mario Praz's *An Illustrated History of Furnishing.*

I also wish to thank The Macmillan Company for permission to quote from "Models and Muses," by James Laver, in *The Saturday Book 15*, edited by John Hadfield, published by The Macmillan Company, 1955, and the Historical Society of Pennsylvania for permission to quote from *A Philadelphia Perspective: The Diary of Sidney George Fisher, 1834–1871*, edited by Nicholas B. Wainwright, published by the Historical Society of Pennsylvania, 1300 Locust Street, Philadephia, Pennsylvania, 1967.

I want to thank the following people, who have been especially helpful in my relentless quest for pictures: Mrs. Ruth Molloy, of Philadelphia; Samuel J. Dornsife, of Williamsport, Pa.; B. A. Sorby, of the Hunterdon County Historical Society, Flemington, N. J.; Mrs. Margaret R. Chatterton, of the Dukes County Historical Society, Edgartown, Mass.; Dr. Joseph A. Baird, Jr., formerly of the California Historical Society, San Francisco; Stanley G. Triggs, of the Notman Photographic Archives at McGill University, Montreal.

For the names of many others I refer the reader to the listing of picture credits, pages 224–230.

I am an amateur photographer; the darkroom magic of two professionals, E. Richard Levy and Frank Speck, made my pictures printable.

J. M.

CONTENTS

"We must never regard buildings as materials shaped one way or another; they are the crystallizations of great dreams of a nation, of a time."

—WILHELM PINDER, 1911

CHAPTER 1

How to
Think about Houses

"But the surest test of the civilization of a people afforded by mechanical art, is to be found in their architecture, which presents so noble a field for the display of the grand and the beautiful, and which at the same time is so intimately connected with the essential comforts of life."

—WILLIAM H. PRESCOTT,
History of the Conquest of Peru, 1847

Nonsense and Sense of Architectural History

On May 11, 1831, Alexis de Tocqueville, a twenty-six-year-old official in the French Ministry of Justice, landed in New York. In his celebrated book, *Democracy in America,* he described one of his first impressions:

> When I arrived for the first time at New York, by that part of the Atlantic Ocean which is called the East River, I was surprised to perceive along the shore, at some distance from the city, a number of little palaces of white marble, several of which were of classic architecture. When I went the next day to inspect more closely one which had particularly attracted my notice, I found that its walls were of whitewashed brick, and its columns of painted wood. All the edifices that I had admired the night before were of the same kind.

From this small incident De Tocqueville drew the large conclusion that democratic societies produce more works of art of less merit than aristocratic societies.

De Tocqueville's observation contains a cluster of misconceptions that are still quite common today. Marble is scarce and costly in the vicinity of New York; brick and wood are plentiful and cheap, and they make good building materials that will last for centuries. De Tocqueville here applied the false standard of "pecuniary beauty," which regards things as "beautiful" if they are expensive—a belief exposed by Thorstein Veblen in *The Theory of the Leisure Class,* published in 1899. De Tocqueville also anticipated an unsound modern argument that claims that forms must be "true to material." The only natural form of marble is rock; the only natural form of wood is a tree. Art is, by definition, artificial. There is nothing wrong with using wood to make a classic column. De Tocqueville was also unaware that the marble columns and entablature of classic Greece copied the timber forms of earlier Greek temples.

Another fashionable fallacy about architecture is the formalistic view. The formalists consider buildings as abstract arrangements of geometric shapes like cubes and cylinders. Formalists also wrote those textbooks of art history in which diagrams with triangles or ellipses are printed over dim photographs of Old Master paintings. They would have you believe that the builders and artists of past times worked according to a theory proposed by art critics in the early twentieth century. The distinguished British historian James Laver has explained the formalist fallacy in plain words: "A generation ago it was the fashion to declare that we should not look for any meaning in a picture, we should be content with its 'significant form.' An artist was praised for painting his mother as if she had been a piece of cheese. But the human mind is strangely recalcitrant to such theories. It persists in taking an interest in the 'subject' of a picture." In the nineteenth century "every picture told a story." Victorian architecture was also designed to convey "meaning."

Americans are devoted to a fallacy called presentism. The "presentists" look for real or fancied resemblances to here and now in the arts of other places and times. For instance, they declare that African sculpture is important because some African masks influenced certain paintings of Picasso, but they make no effort to understand African culture. This is, of course, a foolish approach to history. The arts of the past must be viewed and valued on their own terms.

Another false theory is the mechanistic view of architecture, which claims that form is determined only by technology. For example, mechanistic theorists think that the Byzantines built domed churches because they had just found out how to construct domes. Actually, it happened the other way around: In Byzantine theology the church is heaven on earth, and architects developed the dome to represent the heavenly vault.

A related fallacy is an oversimplified notion called functionalism. It is summarized by the slogan "form follows function," which is credited to the American architect Louis Sullivan (1856–1924). Aristotle said it first, over two thousand years earlier. Form does indeed follow function, but what is the function of a building? Is it just to keep out the cold and the rain? This is only part of the truth. Almost every man-made object also serves as a symbol, a message, an "image of conviction," in the words of art historian Alan Gowans. The home is the largest, the most important, and the most permanent object a man acquires in his lifetime. It is his self-image; it marks his place in society.

M. de Tocqueville, who was so patronizing about the wooden Grecian houses, wore a black suit, white shirt, silk cravat, stickpin, and signet ring with his family arms to manifest his status as an aristocrat and magistrate. The man who lived in the wooden house with the classic columns signified that he was a substantial citizen of the republic. Houses are like clothes; both are shelters for the body which proclaim the owner's status. The history of architecture may be regarded as a branch of the history of costume—or vice versa.

The Mystery of Style

The word "style" is derived from the Latin *stilus,* "a writing tool." It first denoted the character of a man's handwriting, then his distinctive way of expressing himself by the written word. From literature the concept of style spread to the "sister arts," from an individual to entire nations, from a moment in time to decades and centuries.

Art historians study the marks of a style in their special fields, which may be painting, architecture, porcelain, or coins. It has long been known that all the visual arts of a given place and time share a family resemblance of style. The more perceptive historians have also noted striking parallels to the literature and music of the same era. I will give only one example. Here is a description of the house pictured on pages 114–115, written in 1869, a year after the mansion was completed:

> Passengers over the New Haven railroad have noticed a magnificent structure of granite on the outskirts of Norwalk. . . . It might be two country seats of English noblemen rolled into one, or it might be a palace of Ismail Pasha. It is the country residence of LeGrand Lockwood, chief partner in the firm of Lockwood and Co., bankers and brokers, who went under in the Wall Street hurricane.
>
> A wide avenue, embowered with trees and skirted with sumptuous dwellings, stretches for two miles from the railroad station to the heart of town. . . . Halfway between each terminus are three gates of iron which open into the grounds. . . . Beautiful lawns are traversed by gravelly walks, and studded with snowy urns and mythological ideals.
>
> It is a wonder of architecture. . . . Its bright walls sparkle in the sun, towers and spires blend gracefully with its slated roof, and fairy rays of gilt kindle its crest with glory.

It should be apparent that this grandiloquent prose is the counterpart of the lavish architecture. The Lockwood mansion's great Marble Hall also recalls the famous Victorian song "I Dreamt I Dwelt in Marble Halls."

We now realize that the arts are also in accord with what we call life-style—the way people stand, sit, move, walk, dance, talk, sing, dress, eat, drink, court, and behave. To explain this enigmatic omnipresence of style it is sometimes said that art and architecture reflect "the spirit of the time." There is a flaw in this reasoning, though: The spirit of the time does not exist apart from these manifold activities; it is their sum total. The next four pictures demonstrate style in the Victorian environment.

Two fashion engravings show the change of style within a decade:

HOME AND EVENING DRESSES.

1869. The marble fireplace, the mirror and sconce, the chair, and the graceful gowns display the rounded French style. Houses of this period are discussed in Chapter 5.

1879. The jagged, zigzag patterns of the furnishings and dresses belong with the Queen Anne houses described in Chapter 6. Note that the upright stance of the women is in complete contrast to the pliant poses of the slope-shouldered ladies in the scene of 1869.

Fig. 1.—1190—Roselle Demi-Train, 30 cts. each size. 1197—Mathilde Overskirt,
30 cts. each size. 2617—Mariana Basque, 25 cts. each size.

Fig. 2.—1190—Roselle Demi-Train, 30 cts. each size.
2440—Gwendolen Polonaise, 30 cts. each size.

REDMAN & KENNY, N.Y.

Stylish House Dresses.

Two pictures of Victorian children's rooms, twenty-nine years apart:

"Good Morning," 1869. The arched fireplace, the vase and clock, the crib and chair, the carpet and canopy, the curls of the child and hair of the dog, all share the distinctive curves of the period.

The Nursery.

"The Nursery," 1898. The plain Colonial Revival dresser and white painted wooden mantelpiece are in accord with the simple clothes and hairstyles. Note the Oriental vase on the mantel and the baby's Japanese doll.

"The Battle of Styles"

The history of art and architecture has long been told in terms of a succession of styles. The present study also deals with styles because this is a convenient way to present a complex record, but the differences between styles must not be overstated or overrated. All houses within Western civilization share a common tradition and character which far outweigh any changing styles of place and time. The person who reads this book only to learn the names of styles and how to attach labels to buildings is wasting his time.

The history of nineteenth-century architecture has often been described as a battle of styles. Coined by an English architect in 1860, the phrase referred mainly to controversies over the design of certain public buildings in Britain. It should not be taken literally. Throughout Victorian America the various architectural styles flourished in peaceful coexistence. We know that American architects and builders often submitted to their clients alternate designs for a house, of which the ground plan was the same and only the stylish facades varied.

"Man goeth to his long home." Gothic and Grecian side by side in Woodlawn Cemetery, New York.

FRONT ELEVATION

FRONT ELEVATION
SCALE

Italianate and Greek Revival versions of the same design.
The latter was chosen by clients in Philadelphia and
Pottsville, Pennsylvania.

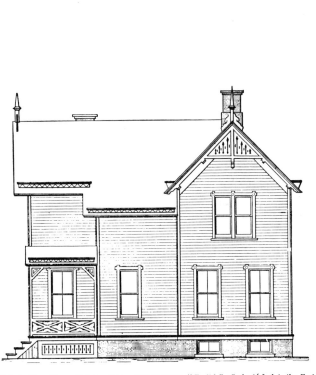

Study in Cheap Frame Houses.—Fig 2.—Side Elevation, " English."—Scale, ⅛ Inch to the Foot.

Study in Cheap Frame Houses.—Fig. 7.—Side Elevation, " English," with Tower.—Scale, ⅛ Inch to the Foot.

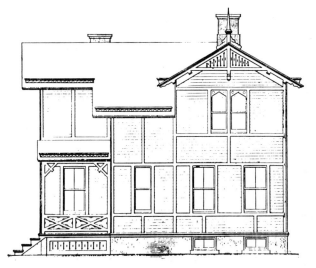

Study in Cheap Frame Houses.—Fig. 5.—Side Elevation, " Swiss."—Scale, ⅛ Inch to the Foot.

Study in Cheap Frame Houses.—Fig. 11.—Side Elevation, " French."—Scale, ⅛ Inch to the Foot.

Four alternative versions of cheap houses to be built in
Newark, New Jersey, in 1879. Cost estimates: "English,"
$1,100; "English" with tower, $1,500; "Swiss," $1,200;
"French," $1,400.

Is There an American Style?

For a long time Americans have needlessly fretted about whether or not there is an American style. In 1853 an anonymous reviewer wrote:

> The nation of the United States patronizes all the styles that have ever been known to mankind, in all ages of the world, and all parts of the earth. Egyptian, Greek, Roman, Saracenic, Cyclopeian, Chinese, Lombard, and all the varieties of Gothic may be found domesticated among us. The American style of architecture has yet to be created. But style, in architecture, is a thing that is more likely to spring from the instinct of the people, who build better than they know, than from a study of other styles, and we think more valuable ideas and hints may be obtained from an examination of our indigenous country houses than by inspecting the architecture of France, England, Germany, and Italy.

Although there were no *wholly* American houses, there were many that were distinctively American, from the shingled cottages of New England and the cobblestone buildings of New York State to the plantations of Louisiana and the ranches of the Southwest. If any of the pictures in this book were shown without captions to a scholar of world architecture, he would be able to identify them as American; the same expert would also be able to match them with pictures of similar houses in Europe and in other countries settled by Europeans.

The nineteenth century was the first age of mass communications, and architecture became the common property of all Western nations. There is no wholly American architecture, but there is no wholly French, English, German, or Italian architecture either. Each of the following chapters opens with a picture of a European building, to show the kind of information or inspiration which was available to American architects at the time. Most of the influence flowed from the Old World to the New, but the last quarter of the nineteenth century saw the beginnings of two-way traffic between Europe and America.

"The Two Nations"

Most books on architecture are top-heavy with royal palaces and aristocratic mansions. As America had no princes of the blood, American historians have concentrated on the residences of wealthy merchants. Does this book give an exact cross section of American homes in the nineteenth century? It does not. It contains more homes of the rich than is justified by their share in the total number of housing units. The annals of the poor are short; they leave few memoirs, few historians have chronicled their lives, and their homes have not been recorded, measured, drawn, painted, or photographed as thoroughly as those of the rich and fashionable. I have, however, made an effort to present a larger selection of ordinary American homes than is customary in books on American history and architecture.

Victorian society was divided into what Benjamin Disraeli called "the two nations"—the rich and the poor. The nineteenth century built notorious slums, but, on balance, the general standard of housing was improved. This was due to technological progress, which produced more houses with better facilities at lower cost. More Americans were also able to own homes because of a new institution, the Building and Loan Association. The members pooled their savings and loaned each other money for the purchase of a home. The first Building and Loan Society in America was organized in Frankford, Pennsylvania, now part of Philadelphia, in 1831. It made its first loan of five hundred dollars to a member named Comly Rich, to enable him to buy a two-story frame house, which is still standing. Millions of Americans were able to become homeowners in this way. By the year 1900 there were 5,386 Building and Loan Societies with over 1,500,000 members in the United States.

As we Sow, we Shall Reap.

Poverty, Squalor, Intemperance and Crime.

Pleasant, Beautiful, Happy Homes.

THE neighborhood here shown is a representation and true type of hundreds of localities which exist all over the face of this fair land. The scene tells its own story—a tale of brutal passion, poverty, base desires, wretchedness and crime.

NOW great the difference! Intelligence, refined taste and prosperity are indicated in these beautiful dwellings. There may be error committed even here, but whatever morality, good sense and culture can do to make people better and happier is to be sought in such homes.

These popular Victorian engravings illustrate a smug attitude and circular reasoning: Nice people have nice homes, and nice homes make nice people. Compare the picture of the pleasant street with the photographs on pages 54 and 55.

Two photographs by Wright Morris show that the homes of the poor were not without a dignity of their own:

Nebraska

Nevada

Two views of the Victorian city's dark side:

A SWELTERING NIGHT IN NEW YORK—TENEMENT-HOUSE SUFFERERS.—DRAWN BY W. A. ROGERS.—[SEE PAGE 410.]

The scene is grim, though the artist has taken care to
include an attractive woman in light attire.

The photograph conveys the real look, and even the smell, of the slum.

The Bones of a Building

The history of building technology has not yet been written. This book does not attempt to fill the gap, but a few remarks on this important and neglected topic are in order.

The nineteenth century developed several new structural systems, including the cast-iron modular system of construction and the steel skeleton, which were used only for public and commercial buildings. Only one of the new systems was applied to the building of homes. This was the wooden balloon frame, first used in Chicago in the 1830's and still the most common method of home construction in America. The balloon frame consists of thin, upright studs nailed to horizontal joists and diagonal braces. It replaced the traditional house frame of heavy posts and beams fitted together by mortise and tenon. A few men and boys who knew how to handle saw, hammer, and nails could put up a balloon-framed house in a few days. The older and slower system had required the labor of skilled housewrights.

The artist has dressed the workers in suits, white shirts, collars, and ties to demonstrate the ease of building a balloon-framed house.

BRANCH'S DIAMOND STONE-SAWING MACHINE

The backbreaking and skilled labor of quarrying, cutting, and "dressing" stone was partially mechanized.

Nineteenth-century America was a country with abundant raw materials and a shortage of skilled workers. This meant a high cost of labor: In 1855 a recently arrived English architect was surprised that "ordinary mechanics ask and get two or three dollars for a day's work." Such a state of affairs led to the development of laborsaving devices. American inventors revolutionized the preparation of the three traditional building materials—stone, brick, and wood—before they were brought to the building site.

21

GARD'S BRICK MACHINE AND TRANSPORTING APPARATUS

The ancient craft of brick-making—a symbol of slavery since biblical times—became an industry that produced brick in a wide variety of sizes, textures, and colors.

J. A. FAY & CO.'S CENTENNIAL EXHIBIT OF WOODWORKING MACHINERY.

America led the world in the development of steam-powered lumber mills and woodworking machinery.

The Modern Conveniences

The greatest contribution of the Victorian age to domestic architecture has been little noted by historians: It was the supply of ample light, heat, and water to the home.

Lighting went through six overlapping stages during the nineteenth century. As late as 1845 candles were still considered the most convenient domestic light. Lamps burning whale oil or vegetable oil, introduced in the late eighteenth century, were used mostly for close work like sewing or studying. After the discovery of petroleum in 1859 coal oil or kerosine fueled the lamps. The next stage was the lighting of city houses by illuminating gas, piped into the house from a factory. In the eighties the Welsbach light replaced the open gas flame with a glowing gas mantle. Finally, after a hard struggle, gaslight gave way to the electric bulb, which was safer and could be pointed in all directions.

Early in the nineteenth century cooking was still done over an open fire. Cast-iron stoves, burning wood or coal, became common in the forties. Cooking with gas began in the eighties; electric ranges were first exhibited at the Chicago World's Fair of 1893.

Victoria Range is one of the handsomest turned out in our foundry. Each range has a handsome skirt nickel teapot stand, nickel band around entire stove, nickel panel on oven door, nickel kicker, nickel shaker, nickel knobs and band on high shelf and outside shelf. It's very heavy in every part, damper on top, large flues, dock ash grate, clean-out under oven shelf, ventilator in oven door. Price includes tea shelf but not high pipe shelf.

STOVE NO.	SIZE OF OVEN.	SIZE OF TOP.	PRICE.
7	. .\ .	. .	$17.50
8	. . .\ .	. .	19.40
9			22.75

The well-organized kitchen of the Harriet Beecher Stowe house at Hartford, Connecticut. The author of *Uncle Tom's Cabin* also wrote a pioneering book on household management, *The American Woman's Home*.

"Weighing the Puppy" shows a Texas farm kitchen. The scene was painted in 1884 by a fifteen-year-old boy, Stephen Seymour Thomas, who later became a fashionable portrait artist.

The source of home-heating moved from the living quarters to the cellar during the nineteenth century. The romantic but inefficient open fireplace gave way to the coal-burning furnace in the basement, which circulated warm air to registers or steam to radiators in every room.

1090—FURNACE REGISTERS.

It is characteristic of the Victorian period that the cast-iron door of the furnace and the brass grill of the register were designed as decorative objects.

At the beginning of the Victorian age householders had to haul or pump water from a well or cistern. It took the better part of the century to bring the benefits of piped water, plumbing, and drainage to the average American home.

In 1917 H. L. Mencken published an article called "A Neglected Anniversary." He related that one Adam Thompson, of Cincinnati, had introduced the bathtub to America in 1842 but that the new convenience had been strongly opposed until President Millard Fillmore assured the triumph of bathing by installing a tub in the White House. Mencken's "bathtub hoax" has been reprinted as fact in books, magazines, and newspapers for over fifty years now. Actually, there had been tubs in bathrooms for centuries, mostly in the homes of people who had servants to fetch and heat water. The bathroom with hot-and-cold running water was a nineteenth-century development.

Note that this bathroom of 1890 has the three usual fixtures plus a fourth convenience.

Image and Reality

Painting, sculpture, and architecture are the three traditional "fine arts," as opposed to the "minor," "decorative," or "applied" arts. This is an old-fashioned and unsound distinction, as many people are beginning to realize in this age of "mixed media." This conventional trinity can still help you to understand some basic facts about the visual arts, however.

Paintings are two-dimensional and usually meant to be seen from a single point; a good reproduction can approximate the effect of a painting. Sculpture is three-dimensional and generally designed to be viewed from several directions; it cannot be fairly represented by a single picture. Architecture is distinguished from these arts by the fact that it has both outside and inside; it also has the fourth dimension of time. A building can be experienced only by walking around it and through it and by observing the view, which changes every instant. Architecture works on all the senses: Buildings have shapes and colors, solids and voids, lights and shadows; they have a texture or touch of their own; they have sounds and echoes; they even have a characteristic smell. Buildings also have the fourth dimension of time: They change with the weather, with the time of day, and with the season of the year.

It should therefore be clear that two-dimensional pictures cannot convey the reality of a house. The pictures in this book have been chosen with great care, but they are only marks of printer's ink on paper. I hope that they will make readers want to experience the real thing.

ENGRAVED by J.C. VARRALL: SKETCH'D by T. HIGHAM: DRAWN by J. MARTIN for BRITTON'S ILLUSTRATIONS of F.A.

FONTHILL ABBEY.

DISTANT VIEW FROM S.W.

London, Printed for the Author, April 1, 1823.

C. & C.

"Fonthill Abbey," the fantastic abode of William Beckford, eccentric heir to a fortune, writer of gothic novels. The 225-foot tower collapsed in 1825.

28

CHAPTER 2

The Gothic Mood

"The Gothic Revival owes its rare force to the way in which it reduced all architectural matters to a religious or a moral issue."

—KENNETH CLARK, *The Gothic Revival*, 1928

The Gothic Revival was an English movement of remarkable intensity and endurance. Beginning in the late eighteenth century as a frivolous fancy for sham castles and mock ruins, it became the dominant style of Victorian Britain for more than half a century. Although popular in America, it could never become dominant because it was the very symbol of Old England, from which the United States had broken away. The British Parliament sat in the Gothic Revival New Palace of Westminster, but Congress met in the Capitol, whose name and architectural style evoked the Roman Republic. (The Canadian Houses of Parliament are in the Gothic Revival style to proclaim continued loyalty to the mother country.) The first Gothic Revival public buildings in the United States were churches and schools of the Episcopalian denomination, which was close to the Church of England.

In America the Greek Revival style of architecture was immensely popular in the 1820's and 1830's; in 1835 a visiting English architect could still report from New York: "The Greek mania here is at its height, as you infer from the fact that everything is a Greek temple, from the privies in the back court, through the various grades of prison, church, custom-house, and state-house." Five years later Gothic Revival residences began to rise in America.

Johann Wolfgang von Goethe, a passionate admirer of both Classic and Gothic buildings, said that "architecture is frozen music"; Gothic Revial architecture was so deeply entangled with poetry and history that it might be called frozen literature. The Victorians took a strong interest in the lives of literary lions. American readers knew that Lord Byron's home, Newstead Priory, was an ancient monastery, and that Sir Walter Scott's home, Abbotsford, was a brand-new ancient Scottish castle. America's foremost authors followed these illustrious examples: Washington Irving medievalized his Sunnyside, and James Fenimore Cooper put battlements on his Otsego Hall.

At first American Gothic houses were copied from English architectural "pattern books"; similar volumes by American authors were first published in the 1840's. The most effective popularizer of the new style was Andrew Jackson Downing (1815–1852), a gardener, of Newburgh, New York. Downing's life was in the pattern of the stories by Horatio Alger. Hard-working, enterprising, good-looking and articulate, Downing made himself into a scholar and a gentleman, a successful author and publisher, and the leader in a new profession. He was a famous man when he died in a steamboat fire on the Hudson River at the age of thirty-seven. Downing's books reveal the literary character of Gothic Revival houses:

> Not a little of the delight of beautiful buildings to a cultivated mind grows out of the *sentiment* of architecture, or the associations connected with certain styles. Thus the style of an English villa will call up in the mind the times of the Tudors, or of "Merry England," in the days of Elizabeth. The mingled quaintness, beauty and picturesqueness of such a dwelling seem to transport one back to a past age, the domestic habits, the hearty hospitality, the joyous old sports, and the romance and chivalry of which invest it with a kind of golden glow, in which the shadowy lines of poetry and reality seem strangely interwoven and blended.

The books of Downing and his contemporaries deprecated the Greek Revival with some ingenious arguments: It was the style of "heathen temples"; its "passionless repose" was not in sympathy with "the American atmosphere or the spirit of this locomotive age." The Gothic style, on the other hand, was Christian, and it was associated with nature.* The Greek Revival house was symmetrical, straight-edged, and painted white, in sharp contrast to the surrounding landscape. The Gothic house was irregular, like the forms of nature; it nestled into the foliage, and it was painted tan or green to "harmonize" with the earth and its plants. It was also "picturesque." This means that the house was designed to make an attractive picture when viewed from various standpoints on the outside. It could also mean that the house was planned and placed to afford attractive views of the landscape from its windows or porches.

Downing was a horticulturist, not an architect. He relied on others to provide the designs in his pattern

---

* The so-called forest theory of architecture claimed that Gothic arches derived from trees. It was first proposed by an anonymous Italian author in 1510 and was still widely believed in the nineteenth century.

A VISIT TO THE HOUSE AND GARDEN OF THE LATE A. J. DOWNING.

When such a man as Downing dies — a man whose life has been eminently useful and beautiful — the world desires to know more of him. Many who in his life-time neither knew Mr. Downing nor felt any interest in the pursuits to which he was devoted, now that he is dead, and especially that his death was so shocking and so sudden, manifest a great anxiety to learn more of his history and of his tastes and pursuits. Many who for years have been in intimate communion with him through his writings, have never, save in imagination, seen his home — the spot which of all others on earth was dear to him. We think, therefore, that at this time the following sketches will be very acceptable; not merely gratifying to that deep and melancholy interest awakened by Mr. Downing's sad fate, but instructive to all who are studying the improvement of grounds.

Mr. Downing's cottage was the first of his designs; and probably it was this that drew him and attached him to the study of architecture, and gave us those writings that have done so much to augment the beauty and comfort of country houses, and which he has left us as an invaluable legacy. This fact alone gives increased interest to the house, and will silence the voice of the critic in regard to any errors or imperfections that may be discovered.

VIEW IN THE GROUNDS.

VIEW FROM THE LAWN.

books, especially on the brilliant Alexander Jackson ...ficient in the Classic, Gothic, ...signed some fine Gothic Re-...few Americans could afford ...er. The Gothic stone-tracery ...wood or iron. "Carpenter ...roughout America for dec-...t the decorative scrollwork, ...in ancient designs of whose ...longer aware. Foundries ...k in many Gothic patterns. ...in America was associated ...lesome and virtuous coun-...ysically and morally pol-...eteenth century there was ...te directions. Millions of ...for the economic oppor-...ber, 1847, Sidney George ...phia lawyer, wrote in his ...nnot live among farmers ...u leave the neighborhood ...arbarism."* At the same ...ring city dwellers moved ...the Victorian city was ...alling environment. ...ies and workshops; coal ...e meals. The steam and ...o the cores of the towns. ...ies, and a layer of soot ...ing cleaning after the ...the housekeeper's an-...ht. Trash and garbage ...curb until they were taken away in open carts and burned at open dumps. On the crowded down-town streets the pedestrian was harried by the din of iron-rimmed wheels, the clatter of hoofbeats, and the splatter of horse manure.

At first only affluent business and professional men who kept horses and coachmen could work in town and dwell in the country. Around 1850 the introduction of

---

* One month later, a European radical, Karl Marx, wrote about the same kind of migration in *The Communist Manifesto*: "The bourgeoisie has greatly increased the urban population as compared with the rural, and has thus rescued a considerable part of the population from the idiocy of rural life."

SPECIAL ORDERS ARE WELCOME

The Book Corral
621 MAIN ST.
CANON CITY, CO 81212
(719) 275-8923

16-Sep-02   10:06 AM
Clerk: Admin Register # 1

Trans. #19546
    * - Non Taxable Items

044022425X 1 $7.99 $7.99
  DRUMS OF AUTUMN
0486412520 1 $16.95 $16.95
  Victorian Home in America
Total Items: 2
        Sub-Total: $24.94
    Tax @ 6.400%: $1.60
          Total: $26.53
  Total Tendered: $40.00
      Change Due: ($13.47)

Payment Via:
CASH $40.00
  Change (Cash)   ($13.47)

275-8923 - HOURS 9:30 TO 5:30 MON-SAT

the horsecar enabled many more people to live in the suburbs. The commuter railroad and the electric trolley car completed this pattern of living. In 1872 the author of *Suburban Home Grounds* wrote: "We believe this kind of half-country, half-town life, is the happy medium, and the realizable ideal for the great majority of well-to-do Americans." He dedicated the book "to the memory of A. J. Downing."

The simplest kind of Gothic cottage, sketched by George Platt, somewhere in the Hudson Valley. Platt was New York's leading "*decorateur*" in the forties and fifties; he furnished "everything connected with the interior ornamental work of houses" at "immense prices."

BELMEAD.

One of America's first and finest Gothic Revival mansions was Belmead, in Powhatan County, Virginia, designed by Alexander Jackson Davis in 1845. It was admired for having "almost every kind of window used at the period to which the style belongs—the triple lancet, the arched, the square headed, the bay, the oriel, and the triangular." A sixty-foot tower "bestowed an air of originality and boldness." This was the estate of Philip St. George Cocke, a noted agronomist and Confederate general; he committed suicide at Belmead during the Civil War. Since 1897 the mansion has housed a school.

The great romantic actor Edwin Forrest designed his romantic Font Hill, a castle of six interlocking octagonal towers, overlooking the Hudson at Riverdale, New York. He borrowed the name from Fonthill Abbey (see the frontispiece of this chapter), though he wrote that Beckford's folly "looked like a church turned into a drawing room by a crazy bishop." Forrest moved to the castle in 1849, but his wife did not join him. After a most sensational and expensive divorce trial the actor sold Font Hill to an order of nuns for one hundred thousand dollars. It is now the library of Mount Saint Vincent College.

Alexander Jackson Davis also built this castellated mansion at Tarrytown, New York, for the Brooklyn merchant John J. Herrick. It was a fine home for a family with eleven children. The house has been destroyed.

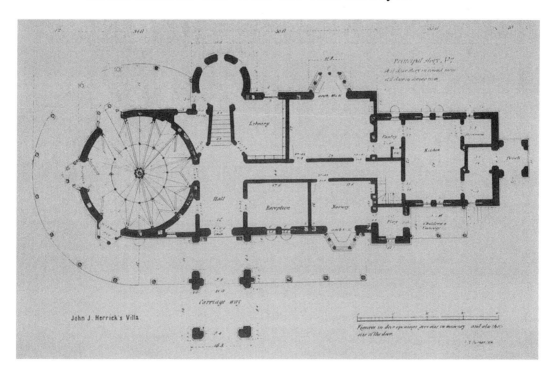

John J. Herrick's Villa.

Lyndhurst, at Tarrytown, New York, the finest Gothic Revival house in America. This view is toward the Hudson River.

An alcove in the dining room.

Lyndhurst is Alexander Jackson Davis's masterpiece. He designed it in 1838 for William Paulding, a former mayor of New York. The villa of white marble was then known as The Knoll or Paulding's Folly. Twenty-six years later Davis doubled the house's size for a new owner, the merchant George Merritt. An account of the seventies delights in enumerating the Gothic features:

> The eye is charmed by the picturesque effect of towers, canopied turrets, gables, and crotched pinnacles; and also with the pleasing variety afforded by the stained glass windows. . . . The arcaded piazza and wide terrace with stone parapet, give shelter and shade, as well as an agreeable promenade. The verandas are richly carved with Tudor flowers and battlements. The Drawing Room has an extensive bay window; a rich ceiling groin, arched with fan tracery, which springs from and supports the columned shafts. . . . The Dining Room is concavo-convex in shape with diverging ribs and ramified tracery. . . . The spacious Library is lighted by a lofty window; the roof is carved, foliated timber, twenty-five feet high in the centre. . . . The Tower surpasses any construction of the kind in America, and is not excelled in England.

In 1880 Lyndhurst was purchased by the financier Jay Gould, and it remained in the Gould family until 1961. The mansion is now owned by the National Trust for Historic Preservation and is open to the public. Lyndhurst is furnished with the possessions of the three families who lived here, including "Gothic" furniture designed by the architect. The photograph shows the drawing room, with the Merritts' furnishings, in the 1870's.

39

Kingscote, at Newport, Rhode Island, has an unusual distinction: It is the work of two leading architects of different generations. Richard Upjohn designed this wooden villa, painted to look like a house of stone, in 1841. Forty years later Stanford White added the shingled wing on the left, with a famous dining room finished in wood, glass bricks, and cork panels.

The entrance hall of Kingscote. The house was built as a summer home for Noble Jones, of Savannah, Georgia.

The Green-Meldrim house of 1856 in Savannah, Georgia, displays crisp Gothic ornament in wood and cast iron.

This drawing of the entrance hall was made in 1864, when the Green-Meldrim house served as General William Tecumseh Sherman's headquarters.

AN ENGLISH COTTAGE.

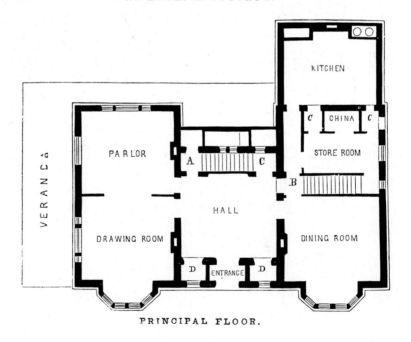

PRINCIPAL FLOOR.

A cottage at Brunswick, Maine, designed by Gervase Wheeler, an English-born architect and author of successful books on home-building.

Nathaniel Virgin, a housewright, of Cambridge, Massachusetts, built this unusual cottage, which has the best of both worlds: Grecian columns and Gothic arches.

FRONT ELEVATION.

A color lithograph from John Riddell's *Architectural Designs for Model Country Residences* (1864), the handsomest and rarest of the Victorian pattern books, and (opposite page) floor plans.

Riddell was a Philadelphia architect who cited the Bible in his preface:

> It is not the intention of the author to give to the reader the idea that he may dispense with the services of an architect in consulting this book. . . . We have two cases given in Holy Writ where two great buildings were commenced. The first one is the Tower of Babel, in the construction of which we cannot learn that any architect was employed, and where all came to confusion. The other was the Temple

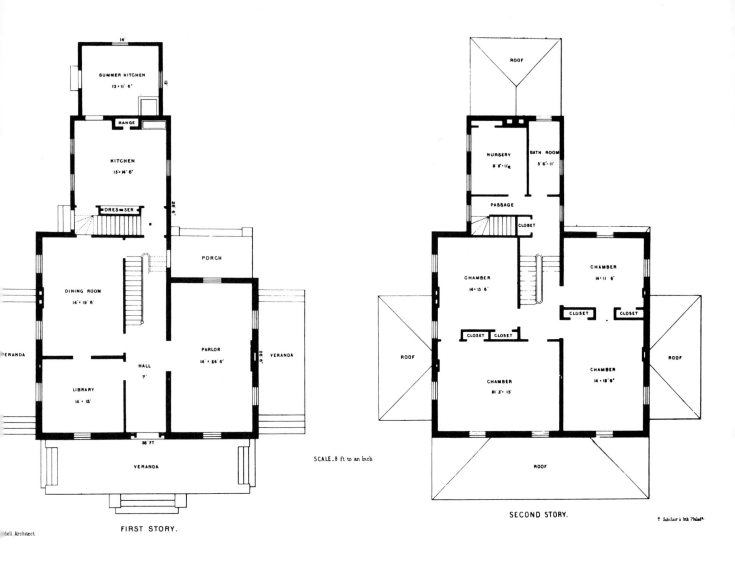

FIRST STORY.

SCALE—8 ft to an inch

SECOND STORY.

T. Sinclair's lith. Philad.

dell. Architect

built by Solomon, who, in wisdom, the world has never seen an equal, but yet he did not think himself wise enough to do without the services of an architect, and his Temple was completed, and became celebrated for magnificence and grandeur.

This Gothic cottage of brick, with iron window-heads, wooden tracery-work, slate roof, terra-cotta chimneys, and four marble mantels, was built by Riddell for five thousand dollars.

45

Three examples of the symmetrical Gothic cottage with "cross gable":

The house of the lawyer Charles G. Sedgwick, in Syracuse, New York, seen in a photograph of the 1860's, was designed by Alexander Jackson Davis. Below is the elaborate coach house. Destroyed.

The homestead of Melville Bell, at Brantford, Ontario, Canada. While vacationing here, his son Alexander Graham formed the theory of the telephone on July 26, 1874. The photograph shows the inventor and his daughter on a visit thirty-two years later.

A farmhouse in central Oregon, abandoned during the Great Depression

The Bowen family settled at Woodstock, Connecticut, in 1638. Henry Chandler Bowen went to New York in 1838 and became a successful publisher. He built his country house, Roseland, on the quiet village green of his native town. The pink Henry C. Bowen Cottage, with its Victorian furnishings, is now owned by The Society for the Preservation of New England Antiquities.

The New York architect Joseph C. Wells painted this view, which is still in the house.

48

John Watkins, an immigrant from England, built this English-looking house at Midway, Utah, of red-painted adobe (sun-dried brick), trimmed with white sandstone blocks and wooden scrollwork. The two symmetrical wings and twin gables are especially appropriate: Watkins was a Mormon bishop with two wives.

Carpenter Gothic designs in western New York State:

The vergeboard of a cottage at Sinclairsville

The house of Amariah Atherly, a potash-maker, at Ashville

The Clark house, Oldwick, New Jersey, next door to the
Methodist Church

Professor Calvin Stowe and Harriet Beecher Stowe, of
Hartford, Connecticut, at their winter home in Mandarin,
Florida, c. 1880

The Gothic villa of Franklin Moore, a grocery and lumber dealer, in about 1870 in Detroit, Michigan. Destroyed.

A Gothic cast-iron veranda and fence, combined with a
gate of classic pattern, in Mobile, Alabama

53

Main Street, U.S.A.: a view in Freehold, New Jersey.

Western settlers planted quick-growing trees and shrubs on the prairie to re-create the look of Eastern towns. This was "Cottage Row," in Cheyenne, Wyoming, in about 1900. The second house from the right was the residence of Governor William Hale; it once had a fountain on the front lawn. Compare this photograph with the ideal view on page 15.

The seaside resort of Cape May, New Jersey, has some of America's finest gingerbread. The towered villa was the summer home of George D. McCreary, a U.S. congressman from Pennsylvania. It is now a church.

Gingerbread was often used to give new style to an older house:

In about 1900 Victorian trelliswork decorated this frame house of the 1830's in Washington, Georgia. The house is now the Washington-Wilkes Historical Museum.

Before-and-after views of a seaside cottage. The jigsaw work included "bathing, fishing, hunting, and other incidents of Nahant life."

The endless variety of the Victorian veranda:

Freehold, New York

Seaville, New Jersey

57

Oak Bluffs, on Martha's Vineyard, Massachusetts, seen here in a photograph of about 1880, used to be known as The Cottage City of America. It still has dozens of fanciful cottages around a Methodist camp meeting ground, painted in many colors and lighted by Chinese lanterns on summer evenings.

In the farming village of Georgetown, New York, stands a square house with strangely notched pillars and three tiers of delicate scrollwork. This was the home of Timothy Brown, a spiritualist. He built it in the 1860's with his own hands and "by the guidance of spirits."

A house "found on the road from Florence
to Prato," drawn by an English architect

CHAPTER 3

The Italianate Image

"At ten in the morning we emerged from the mountains and saw Florence before us, in a wide valley, unbelievably green, and scattered with villas and houses as far as the eye could see."

—JOHANN WOLFGANG VON GOETHE,
Italian Journey, 1786

Few Americans in the first half of the nineteenth century took the "grand tour" of Italy which was so educational for European gentlemen and architects. The Italian influence on American architecture was indirect, by way of British buildings and British books.

Beginning in the 1840's, three distinctive types of Anglo-Italian houses became popular in America. The first was the villa. A villa has been grandly described as "the country seat of a highly cultivated person who feels the necessity of being surrounded by those forms of art which may tend to enhance or bring in relief the beauties of nature." Downing gave a simpler definition: "A cottage is a dwelling so small that the household duties may all be performed by the family, or with the assistance of not more than one or two domestics; a villa is a country house requiring the care of at least three servants."

The British and American villas were inspired by country houses of Italy. The Victorians found these informal stone buildings enchantingly "picturesque"; to twentieth-century viewers they have an interesting "cubist" look. This was often a result of the Italian custom of adding wings or stories to an old house for centuries.

The Italianate, or "Tuscan," villa in America was carefully designed as an asymmetrical but balanced composition. An L-shaped plan with a flat-topped tower in the angle was a favorite scheme. Arched windows, terraces, balconies, and prominent brackets under the roof were characteristic features of the style, which was also known as Hudson-River Bracketed. There were always porches or verandas, also called by the Italian names of *loggia, ombra* (shade), or *piazza* (a misnomer for a porch; *piazza* is the Italian word meaning "town square").

The Italianate villa was by far the most influential house type developed during the Victorian era. Almost all later detached American houses have adopted some of its features. The villa was "designed from the inside out"; as symmetry was not desired, the rooms could be scaled and grouped by function. The effect was said to be "elegant variety," and the message of the villa was clearly: "This is the rich but not gaudy home of a gentleman of taste and culture."

A second type of Italianate house was even more

popular in America than in Europe. The house is shaped like a cube; the roof projects several feet and rests on large, decorative brackets. Atop the center of the roof sits a lookout, now usually called a cupola; in the nineteenth century it was also known as a belvedere ("beautiful view"), lantern, or observatory. Most of these handsome, symmetrical homes date from the forties and fifties.

The third type of American Italianate home is the town house, three or four stories high, with a facade of Renaissance design. Speculative builders erected entire rows or blocks of these narrow but deep houses, producing roomy homes at reasonable cost. The brick front wall was often faced with slabs of chocolate-colored sandstone, the famous brownstone.

The New York brownstone house has been the object of changing views on Victorian architecture and civilization. In 1847 a visitor from Philadelphia wrote in his diary:

> Was much pleased in New York. It is becoming a very great place. We drove through the western part of the city where they are now building in a style far superior to anything before attempted in this country. The new houses on the 5th Avenue, University Place, &c., are palaces. They are very large and executed in a rich, massy, ornate style of architecture. The material is brown sandstone which has a fine effect. The interior arrangement and finishing are said to be admirably convenient.

A guidebook of 1869 described residential Manhattan:

> Fifth Avenue from Waverley Place to Forty-ninth Street is a stretch of two miles and a half, the entire length of which is an uninterrupted succession of costly and imposing mansions. The squares on each side partake of the exclusive character of the Avenue itself, affording a space in which elegance and wealth reign almost supreme. There are many noble residences elsewhere in the city, but we nowhere find so extensive and unbroken a phalanx of brownstone supremacy.

Fifth Avenue on a Sunday Morning.

Sixty-five years later Edith Wharton described the Manhattan of her youth in her autobiography, *A Backward Glance*:

> . . . the intolerable ugliness of New York, of its untended streets and the narrow houses so lacking in external dignity, so crammed with smug and suffocating upholstery. But how could I understand that people who had seen Rome and Seville, Paris and London, could come back to live contentedly between Washington

Square and Central Park. . . . This little low-studded rectangular New York, cursed with its universal chocolate-coloured coating of the most hideous stone ever quarried, this cramped horizontal gridiron of a town without towers, porticoes, fountains or perspectives, hide-bound in its deadly uniformity of mean ugliness.

This vivid picture from memory is entirely false in almost every respect. We know from countless records and photographs what Victorian Manhattan looked like: There were parks and squares, statues and fountains; the streets were lined with trees; the houses were dignified with porticoes of varied design; they were not "low-studded" but had twelve- to fourteen-foot ceilings; the roof line of preskyscraper Manhattan was broken by dozens of towers, domes, spires, and steeples. We also have descriptions of New York by nineteenth-century travelers from Europe; these sophisticated visitors usually found the gridiron plan monotonous, but they were much impressed by the attractive and comfortable brownstone houses of Manhattan.

In 1939 another author painted this lugubrious picture of the brownstone house: "At the turn of the stairs near the landing there was usually a niche with a curved top that enshrined an urn or an apocryphal goddess, in marble or plaster. The Victorians, who made no provision in their houses for such incidents of living as play or lovemaking, took care to provide for the eventuality of death, and the goddess's niche was, in reality, the hole in the wall necessary for the passing of the coffin." In reality, the Victorian house provided very well for lovers with loveseat, inglenook, alcove, back parlor, glider on the porch, and summerhouse in the garden; the romance was consummated in the unsurpassed privacy and comfort of the Victorian bedroom and double bed. The story of the "coffin niche" is a hoax—undertakers did not prepare the dead for burial in upstairs rooms.

In the twentieth century many brownstone residences were converted to rooming houses, and some brownstone neighborhoods became virtual slums. In recent years the comforts and delights of the brownstone house have been rediscovered. It is now in great demand as a family home again. The wheel has come full circle.

DESIGN VI.
A VILLA IN THE ITALIAN STYLE, BRACKETED.

This design from Downing's first architectural pattern book (1842) was repeated in many sizes and versions throughout America.

Stafford Place, at Port Hope, Michigan, is a large, wooden midwestern example of 1866. This was the home of W. R. Stafford, a wealthy lumberman; a grandson lives here now.

Residence of JEHIEL READ.
Hastings

A photolithograph of the classic type of Italianate villa in stone at Hastings-on-Hudson, New York, printed in 1860. Note the lady on horseback.

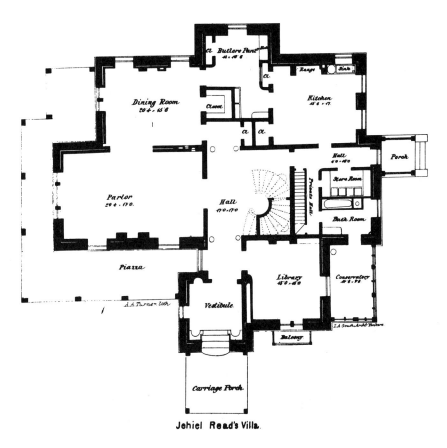

Jehiel Read's Villa.

A watercolor of Camden, near Port Royal, Virginia, designed by the Baltimore architect Norris G. Starkwether. It was painted around 1859, when the planter William Carter Pratt brought his young bride to this great new house on a bluff above the Rappahannock River.

Four years later the tower was destroyed when the Federal gunboat *Freeborn* fired upon the house from the river. The mark of a shell is still seen where it crashed through the wall of the dining room and killed Pratt's infant son. The river facade and veranda are entirely unchanged; Camden is still the center of a working two-thousand-acre plantation today.

In 1863 a Lieutenant Blackford visited Camden, "a prominent object in the landscape," and wrote in his diary:

> The interior of the house is even handsomer than the outside, and is in exquisite taste. It is lighted by private gas-works and has water in every room. Each room is furnished and finished with a different kind of wood—oak, rosewood, mahogany, walnut, etc. The mantles are all of white marble, and the locks and knobs of heavy silver plate. The parlor we were in had the most delightful grand piano, and certainly the most exquisite mirror I ever saw. It was eight feet wide and six high, in an oval frame of rich gilt carving, and on a marble pedestal. The walls of the whole house are covered with beautiful paintings, and in the chambers are some handsome specimens of tapestry.

Every room today looks exactly as it was described by the Confederate officer. Few American homes have remained unchanged since before the Civil War, and Camden is unique: This house has had only two masters since ground was broken in 1856. The present owner is the son of William Carter Pratt, Richard Turner Pratt. He was born in 1886, when his father was sixty-five.

Acorn Hall, at Morristown, New Jersey, was built in 1852 for a young physician, Dr. John P. Schermerhorn. The octagonal tower is far less common than the square type. This photograph of the 1860's shows the white-bearded second owner, Augustus Crane, and his family.

A recent photograph shows Acorn Hall unchanged; it remains a complete period piece of the sixties, with its "double parlors," floral carpets specially woven for the rooms, and furniture by the famous New York cabinet-maker Henry Belter. Four generations of the Crane and Hone families lived here until 1971. The house is now owned by the Morris County Historical Society.

The house of Patrick Barry, a nursery owner, of Roch-
ester, New York; designed by Gervase Wheeler in 1855.
The Gothic building in the background was the office of
Barry's firm.

Summer and winter in the 1890's at Bleak House, a stone villa overgrown with woodbine, on a bluff overlooking Lake Ontario. This was the home of George Beall Sloan, a state senator of Oswego, New York. His great-grandson Sloan Wilson described the house in the novel *The Man in the Gray Flannel Suit* as "a tall Victorian structure with a tower at one end that had been designed to appear even larger and more grandiose than it was."

A Greek Revival house of 1835, remodeled into a towered Italianate villa in 1860 for Joseph Sheffield, financier and benefactor of Yale University. Destroyed.

Mahlon Fisher was a young New Jersey carpenter who designed and built beautiful Greek Revival houses in the 1830's and 1840's; his own home in Flemington, New Jersey, is now called the Doric House. In middle life he moved to Williamsport, Pennsylvania, and became a wealthy lumber dealer. The local architect Eber Culver designed Fisher's new home, a stone villa with towers fore and aft, seen here in 1866, the year it was built. The grounds were ornamented by a fountain, urns, and large statues of "Summer" and "Winter." Destroyed.

74

Outside and inside views from about 1900 of The Willows, near Bristol, Pennsylvania, the house of Joseph H. Schenck, manufacturer of patent medicines. Destroyed.

A group of summer visitors photographed in 1866 on a
Mr. Jessup's veranda in elegant Newport, Rhode Island.
Destroyed.

The Canadian photographer William Notman developed
an ingenious method of making composite portraits: The
MacDuff family, of Montreal, appears to be posing in
front of their home in this 1874 portrait. Destroyed.

Elegant cast-iron statues on gateposts frame The Pink House in Wellsville, New York, built in 1868 for Edwin Bradford Hall, a local druggist. Family traditions often make the dubious claim that "great-grandfather designed our house himself," but in this case there is proof that Hall devised his unique version of an Italianate villa. The Pink House, with its handsome original furnishings and bric-a-brac, is now the summer home of a granddaughter of the first owner.

Italianate villas were often built with superficially
"Gothic" details. Loch Aerie, in Chester County, Pennsylvania, was designed in 1865 by Samuel Sloan for the
collar manufacturer William R. Lockwood.

The Joseph Laird house, in Freehold, New Jersey, is a characteristic example of "Carpenter Italianate."

The Bellamy house, in Wilmington, North Carolina, a
familiar type of Greek Revival Southern mansion with
rich Victorian woodwork

81

Two sunlit Victorian paintings of great houses near San Francisco:

The estate of William Chapman Ralston, at Belmont, twenty miles south of San Francisco. Ralston, a flamboyant entrepreneur, bought the house of an Italian Count, Leonetto Cipriani, in 1864 and had it enlarged into a superb mansion of eighty rooms, where he gave spectacular parties. He later commissioned his architect, John P. Gaynor, to design the eight-hundred-room San Francisco Palace, the most luxurious hotel in the world. In 1875, the year after this picture was painted, Ralston's bank failed, and he drowned himself in San Francisco Bay. His mansion at Belmont now houses a school.

This marvelously precise painting by Joseph Lee looks like the image of the ideal Victorian house and garden, with the family in the phaeton, the proper children at play, the pet deer and the peacock on the grounds. This is Oak Knoll when it was the home of Robert B. Woodward. A Captain Osborn built this house near Napa, California, in the 1860's and was murdered here. Woodward, the owner of an amusement park in San Francisco, bought it from the widow. In later years the Oak Knoll estate became a cattle ranch.

A small Italianate villa by John Riddell, built of stone, with an iron veranda and tin roof, which simulates a striped awning. The ground plan is identical with that of the Gothic cottage on page 44.

This view of Delaware Avenue in Buffalo, New York, shows a fine residential street and its relation to downtown. All these villas have been demolished except the columned Wilcox Mansion (fourth from left), where Theodore Roosevelt took the oath as President in 1901.

Cooke's Row, in the Georgetown section of Washington, D.C., four pairs of handsome villas built in 1868 as a speculative project by the banker Henry D. Cooke. The two end units are in the French style, and the two in the center are Italianate.

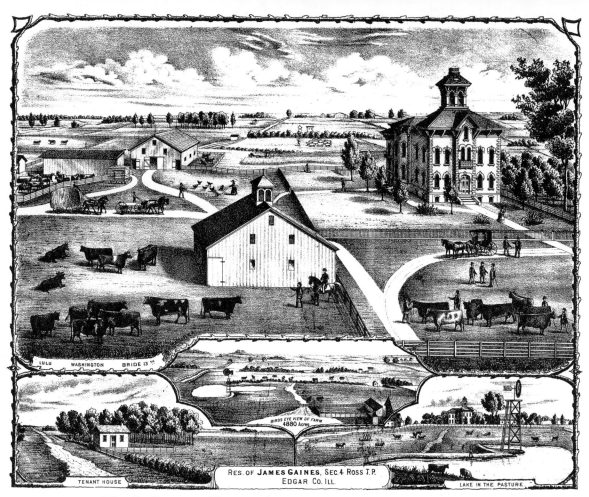

The Italianate villa as a farm

The Italianate villa as a home for the homeless. The Lutheran Home for Orphans and Aged at Germantown, in Philadelphia, is the subject of this endearing painting by an unknown artist.

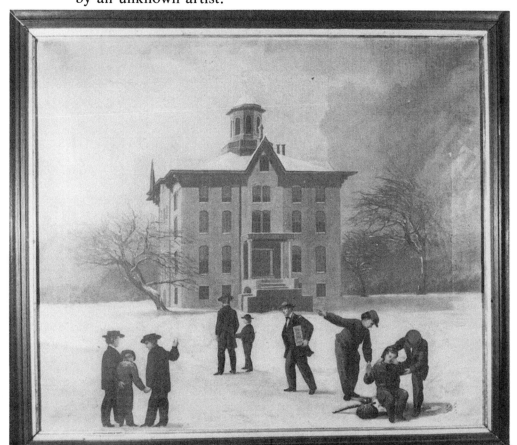

A well-sited villa, built for Daniel Fish, at Greenville,
New York.

Governor and Mrs. Robert O. Fuller ride forth from their home at Cambridge, Massachusetts, c. 1885. Destroyed.

On Cleveland's elegant Euclid Avenue was the house of banker Hinman B. Hurlbut. "A man of fine artistic taste, with ample means, he indulged largely in music, paintings, and horticulture." Destroyed.

Burholme was the Philadelphia estate of the Ryerss family, built in 1859. It is now a park and museum of Oriental art collected by Robert W. Ryerss.

The cupola of Burholme, a hilltop mansion, commands
a fine view.

A row of classic brownstone houses in Brooklyn Heights, New York

On this Brooklyn block is the former home of John Bullard, a broker. In 1872 Edward Lamson Henry painted the portrait of the Bullards in their parlor, which overlooks the East River and Manhattan.

There is a long European tradition of portraying a family group at home. Eastman Johnson was the foremost American painter of such "conversation pieces." "The Brown Family" (1869) shows the New York banker James Brown, his wife, and their grandson in the Renaissance parlor of his town house on University Place. When Brown moved uptown, he had the splendid woodwork installed in his new Park Avenue home.

The entrance to a large Philadelphia brownstone house; this was called The Homestead and was owned by Charles T. Parry, a partner in the Baldwin Locomotive Company

San Francisco has a large number of distinctive wooden houses with facades of Italianate design. Their bay windows and crisp details show to best advantage in this city's strong sunlight and shadow. The elaborate house above was built by the lumberman William C. Talbot as a wedding gift for his daughter. Below is a streetscape in the Pacific Heights section.

The unforgettable "Mourning Picture" was painted in 1889 by Edwin Romanzo Elmer, a spool-silk salesman and self-taught artist. It portrays the Elmers in front of their house at Shelbourne Falls, Massachusetts, and their daughter Effie, who had died at the age of eight.

Elmer's niece Maud wrote that he built his wooden home in 1876 and patterned it after houses he had admired along fashionable Euclid Avenue in Cleveland, Ohio. The second house from the right in the 1865 photograph above was apparently his model. Art historians have convincingly suggested that Elmer painted his daughter with the Lamb of Christ to signify her innocence and death. The symbolism seems to have been accidental: We know from Maud's reminiscences that Effie Elmer did own a pet lamb. This was a popular pose of the time: Two years later, in 1891, another little girl in Massachusetts had her picture taken. Miss Grace E. Allen, of New York, saw this photograph for the first time when I showed it to her in 1972, but she remembers the day when she posed for it with her lamb, Dixie, in front of Sea Rest, her family's home at Edgartown on Martha's Vineyard—eighty-one years ago.

This inaccurate view of the octagonal Mosque of Omar in Jerusalem was published in England in 1849.

CHAPTER 4

Octagons and Orientals

"A Moslem pile in the midst of a Christian land"

—WASHINGTON IRVING, *The Alhambra,* 1832

There have been eight-sided buildings in many countries for thousands of years, including temples, churches, mosques, chapels, baptisteries, chapter houses, castles, forts, guardhouses, tollhouses, pavilions, schools, barns, jails, and tombs; but the octagonal home was the invention of an American. Orson Squire Fowler (1809–1887) was an original of enormous energy, part thinker and reformer, part crackpot and charlatan. Fowler first won fame and fortune as a writer and lecturer on phrenology, the pseudoscience of reading character from skull shapes. He also pioneered in sex education as the author of best-selling marriage manuals.*

Fowler made his contribution to architecture by publishing *A Home for All, or the Gravel Wall and Octagon Mode of Building* in 1849. His principal argument was geometric: Eight walls enclosed more space than four walls inscribed within the same circumference.† He claimed other advantages for octagons: They received more daylight, they were easier to heat, they were cooler in summer by ventilation through a central cupola, they saved steps, they were safer in a high wind.

Fowler also had some sound ideas and a flair for mechanical improvements; he was among the first to advocate hot-and-cold running water in every home, filtered drinking water, speaking tubes, dumbwaiters, and indoor flush toilets to replace the backyard privy. He built his own large octagon at Fishkill, New York, in 1848, but something went wrong with the drainage, and the house was razed as a health hazard in 1897.

A Home for All went through several editions, and other popular handbooks for builders also included instructions on how to construct octagons. Many people were willing to build an eight-sided house, but the habit of living in four-sided rooms was not easily broken. Dividing the octagon into rectangular rooms left odd spaces; no standard solution to this geometric problem was found, and there are hardly two octagons with the same ground plan.

Eight-sided houses are now pointed out as rarities, but thousands were built throughout America, most of them

---

* Fowler married three times, at the ages of twenty-six, fifty-six, and seventy-three.

† A round house is the best solution in this respect.

in the 1850's; hundreds are still standing. There seem to have been no streets or blocks of octagons, though: The eight-sided home, defiant among its foursquare neighbors, was always the choice of an individualist.

The outside of the octagon was adaptable to any fashionable style—Georgian, Greek, Gothic, Italian, or French. Longwood, at Natchez, the greatest octagon in America, was also the grandest example of a fashion that is somewhat outside the mainstream of American tradition, the Oriental, or Moorish, style.

Unlike the British and the French, nineteenth-century Americans had few direct contacts with the Orient. They learned about Islamic arts and civilization through European books. Still, a surprisingly large number of Orientalizing buildings were erected in Victorian America, including synagogues, theaters, clubs, hotels, and Turkish baths. The symbolic meaning of the Oriental style in America was "pleasure," often with an undertone of voluptuous delights; Washington Irving could not look at Moorish architecture "without feeling the associations of Arabian Romance, and almost expecting to see the white arm of some mysterious princess beckoning from the gallery, or some dark eye sparkling through the lattice."

There were only a handful of entirely Oriental residences, but many homes sported some Moorish details, like horseshoe arches or an alcove with arabesques. Oriental styling was also popular for greenhouses and garden pavilions or kiosks. Wealthy men furnished salons that recalled Lord Byron's verses:

> And round her lamp of fretted gold
> Bloom flowers in urns of China's mould;
> The richest work of Iran's loom
> And Sheeraz' tribute of perfume,
> All that can eye or sense delight
> Are gathered in that gorgeous room.

Even middle-class Americans could afford a "Turkish corner," where a few hangings, a rug, a divan, and a water pipe lent an exotic touch to the parlor. In the 1890's a mail-order firm that sold taborets for as little as ninety-eight cents also offered advice on "Moorish style" decorating: "It is wonderful how a little taste combined with judicious expenditure of money can transform a room into a palace."

Eight members of the Pickens family pose in front of their eight-sided home near Ottawa, Illinois, in about 1905. The house was built in 1856 and had wedge-shaped rooms around a spiral staircase. Destroyed.

This mansard-roofed Pennsylvania octagon still stands.

RESIDENCE OF JOHN C. BOORCE, J.P. SURVEYOR & CONVEYANCER.
KULPSVILLE, MONT CO PA.

The William C. McElroy home in San Francisco was built in 1861 of concrete, as recommended in Fowler's book. It was known as The Inkwell. This dramatic photograph was taken in 1906 after the earthquake.

Rebuilt and moved across the street, the McElroy house is now western headquarters of the Society of Colonial Dames. The house was rebuilt in concrete and covered with wooden siding.

The Philadelphia architect Samuel Sloan designed Long-wood, at Natchez, Mississippi, for the cotton-planter Haller Nutt. Sloan wrote: "Fancy dictated that the dome should be bulbiform—a remembrancer of Eastern magnificence which few will judge misplaced as it looms up against the mellowed azure of a Southern sky."

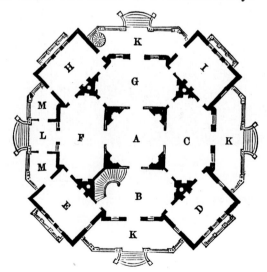

FIG. 20.—PRINCIPAL FLOOR.

The Northern workmen building Longwood left at the
outbreak of the Civil War; the owner died in 1864, and
the unfinished house became known as Nutt's Folly. It
is now owned by the Pilgrimage Garden Club.

106   On a hilltop near Hudson, New York, stands Olana, the home and creation of Frederic Edwin Church, landscape-painter extraordinary. The facades, bright with tiles, were inspired by Persian architecture.

Olana, an estate of over three hundred acres, is the ultimate example of the picturesque: The artist planned every view toward, from, and within the house for colorful effect and visual surprise. Church was a wide-ranging traveler and collector who furnished his home with artifacts from many lands. Olana is now a state park.

The Moorish gazebo at Overlook, a Greek Revival mansion at Macon, Georgia

In 1879 Louis Comfort Tiffany, a son of New York's foremost jeweler, designed the interior of a Fifth Avenue town house for George Kemp, a dealer in drugs. The salon was especially brilliant, with stained glass in the alcove, Indian wood-carving, opalescent tiles and blue glass globes around the fireplace, blue Oriental rugs, and Persian brass lamps hanging from a ceiling of iridescent arabesque design.

The Turkish corner in the New York studio of the painter
J. Wells Champney in the 1880's

This drawing by R. V. Culter was done in the 1920's,
but it captures the character of the Gay Nineties.

THE TURKISH-CORNER CRAZE. THESE ARTISTIC DUST-CATCHERS OF THE EARLY NINETIES WERE SUP-
POSED TO BE TERRIBLY ROMANTIC AND ARE PROBABLY WHAT IS MEANT BY THE PHRASE—"TURKISH
ATROCITIES."

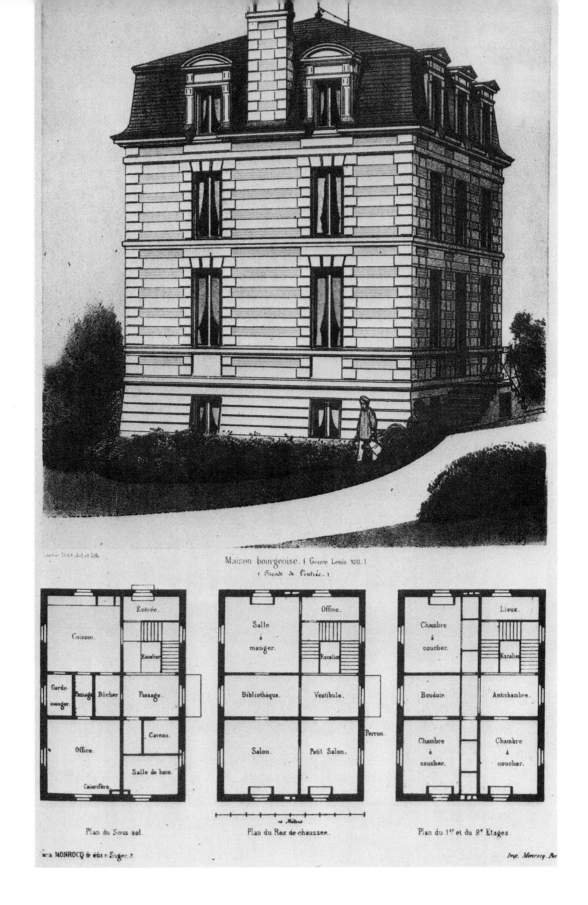

Maison bourgeoise. (Genre Louis XIII.)
(Façade de l'entrée.)

Plan du Sous-sol.   Plan du Rez-de-chaussée.   Plan du 1er et du 2e Étages.

Lithograph from a French book of the 1860's

CHAPTER 5

The French Accent

"Paris is to a man what college is to a boy."

—H. H. RICHARDSON in a letter to his fiancée, 1862

In 1861 the architect Charles Garnier presented his competition-winning plans for the Paris Opéra to Emperor Napoleon III. Empress Eugénie asked: "What is this style? It isn't Greek, it isn't Louis the Fourteenth, it isn't Louis the Fifteenth." The architect replied, "It is Napoleon the Third, your Majesty," an answer both flattering and true.

During the reign of Napoleon III (1852–1870) the city of Paris was renewed on a grand scale, with wide boulevards, impressive public buildings, and elegant apartment houses. The style of Second Empire architecture was a revival of seventeenth-century French Renaissance. Paris became the world capital of art and fashion; two successful international expositions in 1855 and 1867 attracted thousands of foreign visitors to Paris and spread the glory of France to every country. Second Empire buildings rose in cities from Buenos Aires to Budapest, but nowhere was the French impact stronger than in America.

From the late fifties the French mode dominated both public and private architecture in the United States for some fifteen years. This was no revival of the past: The message of the French style in America was "modern" or "fashionable." It is significant that the style went out of favor in America soon after the Franco-German War of 1870–1871, which shattered the Second Empire and damaged the cultural prestige of France.

The Second Empire manner in America has also been called—with a hint of derision—the General Grant style because the major federal buildings were designed in this fashion when Alfred B. Mullett was supervising architect of the U.S. Treasury Department in the first Grant Administration.

The hallmark of the French style was the mansard (with a *d* at the end) roof, named after the seventeenth-century architect François Mansart (with a terminal *t*). It has two slopes, the lower steeper than the upper, and prominent dormer windows. The mansard is both decorative and practical, with more interior space than the attic of a peaked roof. In some European cities it was also used to circumvent height restrictions; if a local ordinance barred buildings of more than four stories, a mansard roof provided a fifth rentable floor.

In America the cross section of the classic French roof was varied in several ways: It could be a concave arc, a

SLEIGHING ON BROAD STREET.

convex bulge, or a combination of both in a graceful S-curve. At the bottom and top of the slope were strongly marked cornices, or "French curbs"; the lower rested on bold brackets, and the upper was topped by cast-iron "cresting."

On the first floor were French windows, reaching to the ground and flanked by louvered shutters. Apart from these characteristic roofs and windows, the French-style house did not differ from earlier Victorian types; the mansard was placed atop homes of basically Gothic Revival or Italianate design. Many pre-Victorian houses were also modernized by adding a stylish mansard roof or tower. In France the mansarded house was a city residence or suburban villa, built of brick or stone. In America the style proved adaptable to city, suburb, town, village, and country; to mansion, villa, cottage, and farm; to every building material from marble to shingles.

The interior of the Second Empire mansion in America is distinguished by strong moldings, plaster medallion, or "rose," on the ceiling, and arched mantelpieces of black or white marble. Within this setting belong boldly patterned wallpaper, flowered carpets, looping drapery, tall mirrors, and curvaceously carved and tufted furniture—the epitome of "High Victorian" elegance.

The French style in America falls within a brief period. In the East a mansard-roofed house was almost certainly built, or remodeled, between the late fifties and the early seventies. There was a time lag of fashion toward the West, and on the Pacific Coast the style lingered on into the eighties.

113

114

The sixty-room mansion (opposite page, top) of the Wall Street financier LeGrand Lockwood, at Norwalk, Connecticut, built 1865 to 1868, was the most lavish American home of its day. Lockwood, who died at fifty-two, lived here for only four years. The building was designed by Detlef Lienau, who had studied architecture in Munich and Paris. Its stately entrance hall (opposite page, bottom) has polished marble columns, an inlaid marble floor, and a richly carved mantel of marble and walnut. At the center of the mansion is a four-story rotunda, lighted from above. From this octagonal hall a sweeping staircase (above) rises to a gallery on the second floor. The Lockwood mansion displays superb craftsmanship in marble, wood, metal, and glass. The fireplace in the music room (left) is flanked by inlaid doors of rosewood, boxwood, and ebony and is surmounted by a Greek goddess etched on glass. The mansion is now the Lockwood-Mathews Mansion Museum.

115

Château-sur-Mer, a massive granite mansion set in fine
grounds at Newport, Rhode Island. Unlike most great
houses of Victorian Newport, this is not a summer villa
but a year-round residence. It was built in 1852 for the
China trader William Shepard Wetmore and was almost
doubled in size twenty years later by his son George
Peabody Wetmore, governor and U.S. senator.

The house is on a grand scale throughout. The architect Richard Morris Hunt designed a library with wooden panels carved in Italy, an impressive billiard room, a French ballroom, a lofty hall, and these unusual stairs, which are painted on the underside. After 118 years in the Wetmore family Château-sur-Mer was left to the Preservation Society of Newport, and it is now open to the public.

Design for a small but beautiful Villa executed in the quiet and charming Village of Rhinebeck on the Hudson.

G. B. Croff. Arch't. Saratoga. N.Y

In 1875 G. B. Croff, of Albany, New York, published a book with the impressive title *Progressive American Architecture*. It contained only designs by the author, including this house for the attorney Andrew Wager.

Croff's villa at Rhinebeck, New York, photographed ninety-five years later. It has since been painted by new owners.

The family of Andrew Allan, a Canadian steamship-line owner, in the drawing room of his Montreal mansion Iononteh in 1871. This High Victorian scene is one of William Notman's finest composite photographs. Compare the lady on the right, holding a baby, with Notman's photographic portrait on page 121.

Andrew Allan's beautiful daughter, Mrs. W. McKenzie, in the conservatory of her father's house. The graceful pattern on the floor is made by the iron grillwork over the furnace in the basement. Mrs. McKenzie was not happy in this hothouse atmosphere: She left her husband and three children and ran away to Winnipeg with a young lover.

The limestone mansion of Alexander Ramsey, governor of Minnesota and U.S. senator, at St. Paul. The house was built in 1872 and remained in the family until 1964, when it was left with its original Victorian furnishings to the Minnesota Historical Society.

Alexander Ramsey, aged eighty-six, wearing a silk hat, on his own front porch; his granddaughter is reading to him.

The home of Edward W. Penniman, a whaling captain, at Eastham, Massachusetts, commands a fine view of the sea. The captain was said to have kept a daily log during the building of this finely detailed wooden house in 1867.

Captain Penniman's bedroom

Riverview Tower, at Marietta, Pennsylvania, overlooks the Susquehanna. It was built in 1860 for Henry Miller Watts, ironmaster and later U.S. minister to Austria.

The summer home of John Price Wetherill, a Philadelphia chemical manufacturer, on the Delaware River at Edgwater Park, New Jersey

The country house of a Mr. Gurd, owner of a bottling
works, on the Back River near Montreal in 1886

Residence of Henry A. Fluck.

The home of an attorney in Flemington, New Jersey; the gable counterpointing the curve of the mansard roof is an uncommon feature.

126

The woodwork, slate, and iron cresting of this house are exceptionally well preserved; it was the home of David H. White, a cabinetmaker, of New Berlin, New York.

The main street of a small town, Clayton, Delaware, shows the diversity of the mansard style.

The mansard by the sea:

Essex County, Massachusetts

Newport, Rhode Island

The mansard on the farm

Mansarded version of an Italianate villa at South Stockton, New York

"The Consecration," a painting by George C. Lambdin
(1865). The setting of this intense scene is a typical
High Victorian home, with glassed-in bookcase, Oriental
rug, tall mirror, and bronze sculpture on the mantel.

The architect Rufus Herrick Dorn built his Los Angeles home in 1887. This photograph was taken about three years later. This home was patterned after a house Dorn had designed in Rochester, New York. When I published a photograph of The Rochester in 1957, it had become an obscure rooming house hemmed in by expressway ramps. The Rochester has since been declared a "cultural landmark" by the city government of Los Angeles and has been moved to a new location.

131

Detlef Lienau designed the eight marble-faced New York town houses on Fifth Avenue as a group. They were completed in 1871 at a cost of over $550,000. Destroyed.

Winslow Homer's engraving "Waiting for Calls on New Year's Day" shows graceful young ladies at a French window. It was a Victorian custom to keep open house for gentlemen callers from 10:00 A.M. to 9:00 P.M.

The most impressive example of Victorian urban planning in America is the Back Bay area of Boston. In 1857 steam shovels began to fill in a muddy tidal bay, and the work continued for over forty years. A residential neighborhood of handsome town houses was built on the "made land," extending westward from the Public Garden for a mile. This photograph of about 1880 shows the eastern end of the Back Bay area. Arlington Street, with its tall French-style brownstone houses, runs along the edge of the Garden. The wide street with the rows of trees down the middle is Commonwealth Avenue, patterned after the boulevards of Paris.

133

A characteristic row of town houses. This is the north side of Walnut Street in Philadelphia in 1888; compare this view with the picture on the top of page 173.

Eastman Johnson's most ambitious conversation piece: the New York stockbroker Alfrederick Smith Hatch and his father, mother-in-law, wife, and eleven children, painted in the library in 1871. The artist was said to have received one thousand dollars for each of the fifteen portraits, including that of the baby, Emily, who was born after the painting was begun. The house still stands on Park Avenue.

"The Chessplayers" (1876), painted by Thomas Eakins, shows the solid comfort of the Eakins parlor in Philadelphia, with the elegancies of bronze clock and Turkish water pipe on the mantel. The three friends are, from left to right, Bertrand Gardel, a French teacher; the artist's father, Benjamin Eakins, a teacher of penmanship; George W. Holmes, an art teacher.

The Eakins home, where the artist lived for fifty-nine years, was the house with the added mansard story. It will be developed as a community center.

LESLIE'S ROW.

A New York reporter wrote this description in 1871:

Philadelphia has but few tenement houses. Each household has its own dwelling, which is its home. The houses are small, but complete. There are two rooms on the first floor, besides a kitchen. On the second floor are bed-rooms and a bath-room; thus making a snug little home for the young mechanic or frugal laborer. It seems, at first, that there could be no improvement on this arrangement, but a great one has been adopted. A single block was set apart for the erection of small houses, and as those who would occupy them would not use carriages, it was proposed that a way for carrying in coal, groceries, etc., should be made in the rear of the buildings, while in front nothing but a flagged sidewalk should be left for the public travel, the whole street being covered with greensward, making a little park for the occupants of the houses.

Leslie's Row, now called St. Alban's Place, with its separation of vehicular and pedestrian traffic, was a pioneering example of good city planning. After more than a hundred years it remains an oasis in a drab neighborhood. The house-proud owners of the fifty-two homes on St. Alban's Place have formed their own civic association. They contribute both labor and annual dues to the planting and upkeep of the common garden; the cast-iron fountains have become urns for flowers. The concept of a fenced park, reserved for the neighbors, derives from the squares of eighteenth-century London; Gramercy Park in New York is an American example.

Illustration showing an English country house, published in 1875

CHAPTER 6

The Nameless Period

"Yes, sir, give an architect money enough, and he'll give you a nice house every time."

—WILLIAM DEAN HOWELLS,
The Rise of Silas Lapham, 1885

The seventies and eighties have a distinctly unfavorable image in our historical consciousness. They are sometimes called the Gilded Age* or the Brown Decades.† There were no dramatic political events, no towering Presidents; it was a time of great population growth in the United States (from forty million people in 1870 to sixty-three million in 1890), of bust and boom in business, of technological progress (Bell's telephone was invented in 1876, Edison's light bulb in 1879).

In the arts the two great world's fairs were significant markers at the beginning and the end of the period: the Centennial Exhibition of 1876, in Philadelphia, and the World's Columbian Exposition of 1893, in Chicago. There is no common name for the complex architecture of this era, though there are labels for the several styles that coexisted during these decades.

The first of these was called the Queen Anne style. It is a misnomer; Victorian Queen Anne houses bear almost no resemblance to the architecture of that English queen's short reign (1702–1714). The Victorian style was an English revival of even earlier picturesque houses of the Elizabethan and Jacobean periods. It began in the late sixties and was soon taken up by American builders who studied English architectural publications.

The American Queen Anne house is one of the most complex habitations ever devised for commoners. It rejected the traditional concept of unity in design, deliberately contrasting shapes, textures, and colors— solid and void, in and out, square and round, light and dark, rough and smooth. The ground plan is irregular, each facade has a different elevation, and the roof, with its intersecting ridges and turrets, is a problem in solid geometry. Each

* The title of a satiric novel by Mark Twain, published in 1873.
† The title of a book by Lewis Mumford, subtitled *A Study of the Arts in America*, published in 1931.

story is usually finished in a different material. The ground floor may be stone trimmed with brick, or brick trimmed with stone; the second story is faced with clapboards or shingles; the third story often features half-timbered gables, topped by a roof of varicolored slate. There are porches, overhangs, bay windows, oriels, balconies, leaded glass, stained glass, plaster relief panels, dormers, turrets, towers, and clustered brick chimneys. Paradoxically, this busy allover pattern created a unity of its own, very much like a patchwork quilt that makes a strong design out of many different fabrics.

Both the exterior and the interior of the house displayed a large amount of elaborate wooden trim, spindlework, and paneling. Gothic Revival gingerbread was sawed out of boards; Queen Anne "millwork" was turned or carved, produced by steam-powered machines. Foreign observers at the Centennial Exhibition marveled at the ingenious design of American woodworking machinery. For example, one Ohio manufacturer exhibited a line of "patent universal wood-workers for planing out of wind, jointing, squaring, smoothing, beveling, cornering, chamfering, tapering, mitreing, rabbeting, tenoning, halfing, panel-raising, tongueing, grooving, hand-matching, rolling-joints, gaining, plowing, serpentine and waved moulding, fluting, beading, ripping, splitting, cross-cut sawing, straight, circular, oval, and elliptical mouldings, dove-tailing, etc."

The exterior of the Queen Anne house sometimes bordered on the bizarre, but the interior provided solid comfort. A distinctive feature of the style was a large English type of hall, with fireplace and open staircase, which served as a living room. The fireplace and flanking seats were often in a cozy, tile-floored recess, called an inglenook. The desired effect of the Queen Anne house is "artistic"; the self-image of the style is summed up in the last sentence of the bumptious "history" on page 142.

The Log Cabin

The Colonial House

The Nondescript

Gothic

The Classic Mansion

Italian

A Modern House

The Mansard Roof

DOMESTIC ARCHITECTURE IN AMERICA

FIRST the Log Cabin; then the Colonial House, which was built before and for some time after the War of the Revolution; then the Classic Mansion early in the present century, which sprang from an ambitious attempt to copy the style of public buildings; later the Gothic and Italian obtained some recognition, and about the same time (1830 to 1840) arose the great Nondescript—the square box, modeled after a packing-case, which every rough carpenter could build,—and he has built it, unfortunately, from one end of the land to the other; next (about 1860) appeared the Mansard Roof, a modification of the box style, simple and easy to construct and therefore popular with the carpenters, who urged them upon thousands of owners; and last the Modern House, designed by the architect and not by the mechanic, having beauty and unity of design and intelligent provision for the comforts, elegancies and refinements of life.

The formally educated architect emerged during the seventies. The first department of architecture at an American college, the Massachusetts Institute of Technology, opened in 1868, and the first successful architectural magazine, *American Architect and Building News*, began publication in 1876. The changes in style and spirit are nicely described in the novel *The Rise of Silas Lapham*. The hero, a newly rich paint manufacturer, has bought a lot in the fashionable Back Bay of Boston and has engaged the services of an architect:

> Colonel Lapham's idea of a house was a brown-stone front, four stories high, and a French roof with an air-chamber above. Inside there was to be a reception room on the street and a dining-room back. The parlours were to be on the second floor and finished in black walnut. . . . The chambers were to be on the three floors above, front and rear. . . . Black walnut was to be used everywhere. The whole was to be very high studded, and there were to be handsome cornices and elaborate centrepieces throughout.
>
> These ideas he had formed from the inspection of many buildings which he had seen going up. . . . He was confirmed in his ideas by a master builder who had put up a great many houses on the Back Bay as a speculation, and who told him that if he wanted a house in the style, that was the way to have it.
>
> The beginnings of the process by which Lapham escaped from the master builder and ended in the hands of an architect are so obscure that it would be almost impossible to trace them. But it all happened, and Lapham promptly developed his ideas of black walnut finish, high studding, and cornices. The architect was able to conceal the shudders which they must have sent through him. He was skilful, as nearly all architects are, in playing upon that simple instrument Man.[*]

* The author's son, John Mead Howells, became a noted architect.

"Have the entrance-story low-studded and your parlours on the next floor as high as you please. Put your little reception-room here beside the door, and get the width of your house frontage for a square hall, an easy low-tread staircase running up three sides of it. I am sure Mrs. Lapham would find it much pleasanter. . . . Then have your dining room behind the hall, looking on the water. . . . That gets you rid of those long, straight, ugly staircases"— until that moment Lapham had thought a long, straight staircase the chief ornament of a house —"and gives you an effect of amplitude and space."

Closely related to Queen Anne was the Eastlake style, named after the English author of *Hints on Household Taste*, published in 1868 and soon reprinted in America. Charles Locke Eastlake promoted a peculiar kind of furniture and interior decoration which were the deliberate opposite of the voluptuously rounded French style. It was squarish, notched, jutting, and associated with earnest notions of "reform," "sincerity," and "honest craftsmanship." Gothic Revival furniture had imitated the forms of Gothic Revival architecture. Eastlake furniture reversed this process: Some houses of the period had outside posts, brackets, and incised ornament reminiscent of the Eastlake furnishings inside.

At the same time there was some gentle influence on American houses and furnishings from the Far East. At the Centennial Exhibition Americans first confronted the arts of Japan. Soon Japanese screens and scrolls were recommended to sophisticated homeowners: "They are often far more beautiful than any pictures by our own men, that we with the short purses can lay hands upon."

Distantly related to the Queen Anne fashion was a type of wooden house which had no name at the time. It has since been dubbed Shingle Style, though not all of the homes had shingled walls.

The wooden shingle had been a traditional roofing material for centuries, but European builders very rarely used shingles as siding. In New England, however, shingled walls had been common since the seventeenth century; they proved serviceable along the coast, where the salt air damaged house paint. The Victorian shingled houses were also most popular on the Eastern seaboard. These large, rambling suburban houses and summer cottages had few associations with a European style; they were vaguely felt to be in an American tradition. Perceptive European observers soon recognized them as a distinctive American contribution to residential architecture. These ample, informal houses are now admired for their "modern" character and interesting "open" plans.

The last style of these decades was named after Henry Hobson Richardson (1838–1886). No other American architect before or since Richardson made such an immediate impact on the American scene. He was an original designer and a forceful personality, but his overwhelming success is difficult to account for. His highly personal style was partly inspired by the Romanesque architecture of early medieval France, which lacked historical connotations for nineteenth-century America.

Richardson was primarily an architect of monumental public structures (he said that the ladies were so difficult to please that he preferred to erect public edifices, in the building of which he dealt with committees of men); even his small buildings look monumental. He designed a small number of distinguished wooden houses and a few masonry mansions in his "public" style. This fortresslike manner would not seem to be particularly suited to homes. In 1891 the critic Montgomery Schuyler wrote about the house that Richardson had built for the Chicago manufacturer J. J. Glessner: "It ceases to be defensible, except, indeed, in the military sense. The whole aspect of the exterior is so gloomy and forbidding and unhomelike that but for its neighborhood one would infer its purpose to be not domestic but penal."

After Richardson's death at the age of forty-eight, his successors and many imitators built "Richardsonian Romanesque" houses by the thousands. Lacking the departed master's touch, the houses are grim structures of gray or brown boulders. Such a formula had to lead to a dead end. By the time of the Chicago World's Fair of 1893 the style had disappeared as suddenly as it had come.

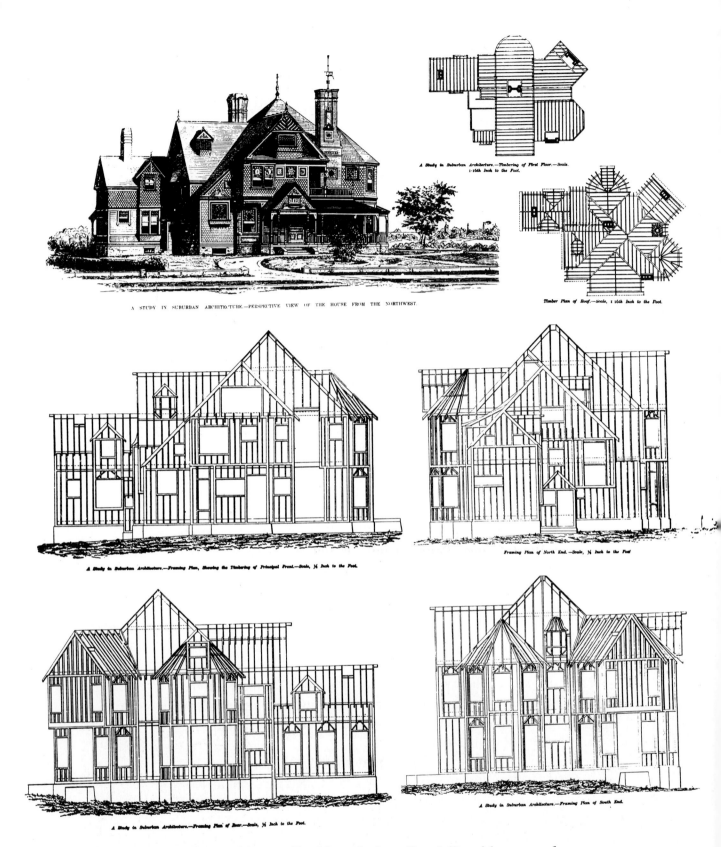

A STUDY IN SUBURBAN ARCHITECTURE.—PERSPECTIVE VIEW OF THE HOUSE FROM THE NORTHWEST.

A Study in Suburban Architecture.—Timbering of First Floor.—Scale, 1-16th Inch to the Foot.

Timber Plan of Roof.—Scale, 1 16th Inch to the Foot.

A Study in Suburban Architecture.—Framing Plan, Showing the Timbering of Principal Front.—Scale, ¼ Inch to the Foot.

Framing Plan of North End.—Scale, ¼ Inch to the Foot

A Study in Suburban Architecture.—Framing Plan of Rear.—Scale, ¼ Inch to the Foot.

A Study in Suburban Architecture.—Framing Plan of South End.

The architects Gould and Angell, of Providence, published these characteristically complicated plans in 1883.

A beach-front house at Long Branch, New Jersey, now serving as a rectory.

The new paint job on the former Ishmael Jefferis home at West Grove, Pennsylvania, is not the original color scheme, but it accentuates the Queen Anne variety.

147

MARK TWAIN'S HOUSE

BUILT 1874   EDWARD TUCKERMAN POTTER, ARCHITECT

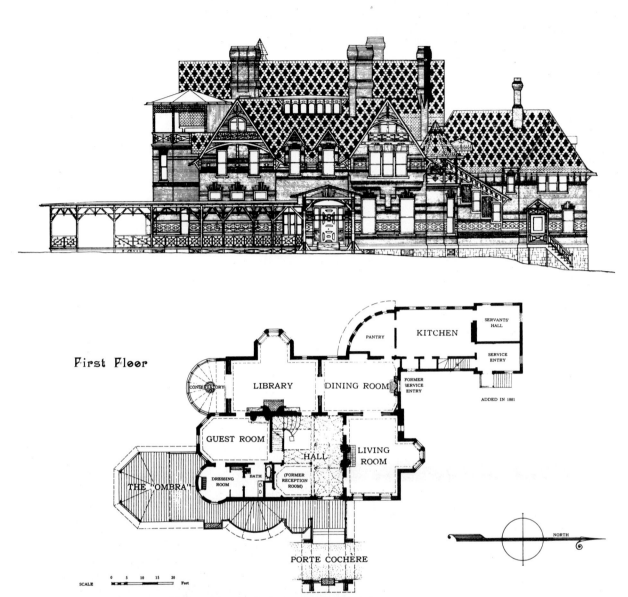

First Floor

These are the bricks of various hue
And shape and position, straight and askew,
With the nooks and angles and gables too,
Which make up the house presented to view,
The curious house that Mark built.

This is the sunny and snug retreat,
At once both city and country seat,
Where he grinds out many a comical grist,
The author, architect, humorist,
The auctioneer and dramatist,
Who lives in the house that Mark built.
                              —Mark Twain, 1877

Mr. and Mrs. Samuel Langhorne Clemens, with Susy, Clara, and Jean, on the porch of their home in Hartford, Connecticut, about 1885. In 1874, when the house was under construction, a Hartford newspaper said: "The novelty displayed in the architecture of the building, the oddity of its internal arrangement, and the fame of its owner, will all conspire to make it a house of note for a long time to come." This prediction has come true.

The library of Mark Twain's house opens into a small conservatory of a pattern popularized by the writer's friend and next-door neighbor, Harriet Beecher Stowe. Flanking the arch are two romantic Victorian favorites: "The Questioner of the Sphinx," by Elihu Vedder, on the easel and the "Medici Venus" on the pedestal.

An unusually delicate Queen Anne design at Edgwater Park, New Jersey

Henry W. Merriam, a shoe manufacturer, of Newton, New Jersey, built his home in 1883; he willed it to the Presbyterian Church.

STAIRCASE AND HALL.

Design for a Queen Anne–style living hall with inglenook and open staircase by the popular architect Henry Hudson Holly, published in 1876.

"The Letter" (1881), painted by J. Wells Champney, shows Mr. and Mrs. Samuel Colgate in their cozy living hall at Narragansett Pier, Rhode Island.

Simple houses with spindlework porches:

Los Angeles, California

Ashland, New York

152

"The Crimson Rambler" (1908), by the Boston painter
Philip Leslie Hale, celebrates the charm of the veranda.

The summer cottage of a Dr. Tucker, a tonic manufacturer, at Oak Bluffs, on Martha's Vineyard, about 1885.
President Ulysses S. Grant was a house guest here.

Residence of W. E. Emery.

Emery left Flemington, New Jersey, as a young man and founded a department store in Kansas City. He retired as a wealthy man and built Rose Lawn, seen here in the 1890's, on the site of his birthplace.

Rambling Rose Lawn today

What is the function of the turrets often seen on corners and porches? Their function was to show that the owner could afford to build a home with decorative turrets.

A view on Avenue I in Galveston, Texas. In the foreground the elaborate Sonnentheil House of the eighties.

This house, pictured in 1886, and the one on the facing
page display the characteristic Queen Anne variety of
materials: stone, brick, clapboard, shingles, half-
timbering, and terra-cotta ornaments. The massive mansion of the New York banker Henry Pearl Talmadge, at
Plainfield, New Jersey, had an unusual lighthouselike
tower. Destroyed by fire in 1969.

The New York architects Potter & Robinson designed the house of Commodore Charles H. Baldwin, U.S. Navy, on fashionable Bellevue Avenue, in Newport, Rhode Island. Inside is an impressive two-story living hall with a balcony around it.

The architect of this Los Angeles extravaganza is not
known. It was the residence of Frederick Mitchell
Mooers, who had struck a gold mine in California.

Hermosa Vista, at Redlands, California, built in 1890 as
the home of David A. Morey, a sixty-six-year-old orange-
grower, was photographed in the 1890's. The owner designed the house himself with some help from Jerome E.
Seymour, a friend who owned a lumber mill. Morey had
worked as a shipwright and mine carpenter, and he
applied the technique of a boat-builder to construct the
original and delightful onion dome. I published a photograph of the house in 1957, and the picture captured the
fancy of a large public; Hermosa Vista has become a
favorite of artists, photographers, writers, and sightseers.

The Nevada silver-mining millionaire Elias Jackson Baldwin and his daughter Anita are portrayed in 1889 on his Rancho Santa Anita, at Arcadia, California. Beyond the lake is the cottage built for his guests in 1881.

"Lucky" Baldwin's guest house, with its original Victorian furnishings, is now owned by the County of Los Angeles and is open to the public. It is known as the Queen Anne Cottage. The architect, A. A. Bennett, actually derived the plans from designs of villas published in French periodicals.

Two views in Port Townsend, Washington, which had its lumber and shipping boom in the eighties:

The home in the foreground was built as the carriage barn of the red house in the background, which is known as Frank's Folly or the Old German Consulate.

The photographer is focusing on the small but fancy cottage that was the home of N. D. Hill, a pharmacist. In the background is the former mansion of George E. Starrett, a builder, named the House of the Four Seasons after murals on this theme inside the tower.

EUREKA.

Samuel & Jos. C. Newsom
Architects
504 Kearny St
Top Floor
San Francisco.
Cal.

FRONT ELEVATION

The architect's elevation of the Carson Mansion at Eureka, California, which has become one of the most famous houses in America

William McKendrie Carson was the owner of redwood forests in northern California. He had his house built in 1884 and 1885 to give employment to the workers in his lumber mills during an economic depression. The mansion was said to include every kind of wood on the world market, brought to Eureka on Carson's own ships.

A historian has called the Carson Mansion "so aggressively frightful as to be enchanting." It is now a club.

The Carson-house interior also displays bizarre design and craftsmanship in wood.

The eighties delighted in stained glass:

The entrance to the home given by William Carson to his
son as a wedding present in 1889.

Salvaging a window from a West Philadelphia house
about to be demolished.

167

Augustus Laver, an English-born architect, designed Canadian government buildings at Ottawa, the New York State Capitol in Albany, and the San Francisco Hall, all with spectacular towers. In 1878 he found a client who desired a house built on the scale to which Laver had become accustomed. He was James C. Flood, a former San Francisco barkeep who had made millions in Nevada silver-mining stock.

Linden Towers, at Menlo Park, California, in a lithograph of about 1880. A dazzling white conglomeration of several Victorian styles, the house became known as Flood's Wedding Cake. Even the stable, in the left background, was a mansion, with its mahogany stalls and silver fittings. Destroyed.

THE COUNTRY RESIDENCE AT MENLO PARK OF
JAMES C. FLOOD, ESQ.

This fantastic house in Galveston, Texas, was built in 1890 by the little-known architect Alfred Muller for the merchant John C. Trube.

VIEW BEFORE ALTERATION.   VIEW AFTER ALTERATION.

VIEW IN HALLWAY AFTER ALTERATION.

In 1878 William M. Woollett, an architect, of Albany, New York, published a book called *Old Homes Made New* in which he demonstrated how to turn plain houses into more stylish residences in the Eastlake manner.

SOUTH-EAST VIEW OF RESIDENCE, RIDGEFIELD, CONN.

Did anyone actually hire Woollett for one of his rebuilding schemes? J. Howard King, Esq., did, and the architect published these before-and-after photographs of King's summer residence.

These Washington, D.C., homes show the typical bay
windows and "cut brick" facades of the Queen Anne
town-house style.

This Philadelphia block is directly opposite the row shown in the photograph on page 134. The deliberate restlessness and variety of the eighties, shown in this 1888 photograph, is in marked contrast to the unified design of the early seventies. The house at the corner is in the "Ruskinian Gothic" style popularized by John Ruskin, the English author of *The Stones of Venice*.

A view, published in 1883, in the town house of Henry C. Gibson, a Philadelphia distiller and art-collector

Nickerson's Marble Palace was built in 1883 for the Chicago banker Samuel M. Nickerson. These photographs, taken in the 1890's, show the formal dining room and an informal bedroom in the mansion. It is now occupied and well maintained by an audio-visual firm.

Every item in Mrs. Vaughan's drawing room in Montreal
in 1893—from lace curtains to tea cozy—proclaim her
to be a genteel lady.

Grasshead, at Swampscott, Massachusetts, designed in
1882 by the architect Arthur Little for his parents. It is
a characteristic large seaside "cottage" of brick and red-
stained shingles, with some whimsical touches that include a shingled "half beehive" over the front door and
tree trunks as porch pillars. Beyond the breezeway on
the right is a lighthouselike tower that served as "a
dressing room for bathers who have been disporting
themselves in the sea at a distance of scarcely 200 feet."

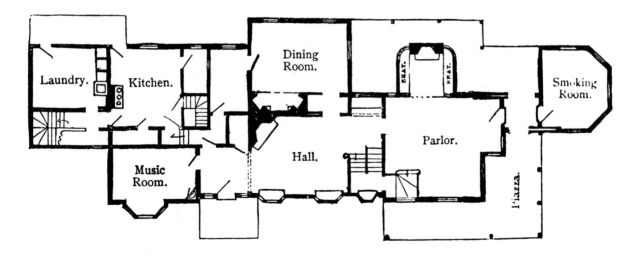

GROUND PLAN.

In 1886 the Meadow Brook Hunt Club met at Oyster
Bay, Long Island, in front of the new home of Theodore
Roosevelt, a lawyer and state legislator. Years later
Roosevelt wrote of Sagamore Hill:

> I had perfectly definite views what I wished in
> inside matters, what I desired to live in and
> with; I arranged all this, so as to get what I
> desired so far as my money permitted; and
> then Rich [the architect] put on the outside
> cover with but little help from me. I wished a
> big piazza where we could sit in rocking-chairs
> and look at the sunset; a library with a shallow
> window looking south, the parlor or drawing-
> room occupying all the western end of the
> lower floor . . . big fireplaces for logs.

"A Friendly Call," painted in 1895 by William Merritt Chase, portrays his wife and a visitor at the artist's shingled summer home near Southampton, Long Island. The airy room, with its bamboo chair, straw matting, and Oriental embroidery, shows the influence of Japan. The painting itself also owes something to the subtle design of Japanese prints.

The shingled Warren Weston house on breezy Chappa-
quiddick Island, Massachusetts

A photograph published in 1886 of the residence of
Travis C. Van Buren, at Tuxedo Park, New York, a
fashionable planned community, designed by the architect Bruce Price. The house is small, precise, and ele-
gantly simple. Life was informal at Tuxedo Park: Gentlemen dressed for dinner in *short* jackets. Price's well-
mannered daughter Emily became Mrs. Edwin M. Post.

A style was born in this room, the library of Henry Hobson Richardson at his home in Brookline, Massachusetts. His biographer wrote in 1888:

> Even at first sight Richardson's library had not the aspect of those rooms filled to overflowing with miscellaneous bric-a-brac which in recent years we have come to know so well. It was just as full and its contents were just as varied, but the general effect was harmonious and restful; there was no rubbish among the things which professed to be works of art, there were no ugly objects of utility, and each item bore witness to the strong personal tastes and the actual material or professional needs of the owner. It was evidently in the first place a room to work in, although it was so charming a room to lounge in that even the casual visitor was loath to leave it.

On the table stands a framed photograph of Richardson in a monk's cowl.

This shingled home of Mrs. M. F. Houghton, in Cambridge, Massachusetts, was one of Richardson's most admired and most imitated designs.

Behind the towerlike projection is the hall, with the characteristic window seat and open staircase.

A Philadelphia house shows the "rock-faced" masonry that was popular in the eighties.

The Tiffany mansion, on Madison Avenue, in New York City. It was designed by Stanford White from a sketch by Louis Comfort Tiffany, who had his apartment and studio on the top floor. Destroyed.

‹ FRONT ‹ ELEVATION ‹

This potpourri of 1888 demonstrates the astonishing impact of Richardson: All of the three public buildings and eight homes shown are in his manner. Note that the late master is the only architect mentioned by name.

The Richardsonian influence in Canada: the house of
Sir George Drummond, president of the Bank of Montreal,
in 1896. Destroyed.

184

DWELLING IN ST. PAUL.
Mould and McNichol, Architects.

PORCH IN ST. PAUL.—Mould and McNichol, Architects.

The mansion of the banker John L. Merriam, in St. Paul,
Minnesota, shows the Richardsonian mannerisms carried
to extremes. It later housed a science museum. Destroyed.

185

CHÂTEAU DE CHAMBORD

GRANDE FAÇADE

A. DUPUIS, Éditeur, 9. rue des Beaux-Arts, Paris

Photographs of historic buildings, like this
one of 1875, became a major influence
toward the end of the century.

186

CHAPTER 7

An End and a Beginning

"Changes in manners and customs, no matter under what form of government, usually originate with the wealthy or aristocratic minorities and are thence transmitted to the other classes."

—EDITH WHARTON and OGDEN CODMAN,
The Decoration of Houses, 1897

The Gay Nineties were a time of great seriousness in American architecture. The education of American architects was now formally modeled after the program of the French École des Beaux Arts. The method of instruction at the École, which had been teaching architecture since 1671, was more than a pedagogic system; it was a solemn ritual. Before they proceeded to modern designing, students were thoroughly drilled in the study of historic styles. Their assignments were of the utmost formality and grandeur; for example, they were told to design "A Presidential Palace for the Capital of a Great Republic" or "A Votive Church in a Pilgrimage Place of Note." Their solutions were almost always perfectly symmetrical in plan and elevation.

The most talented young Americans competed for the honor of studying in Paris, but is was not necessary to cross the Atlantic to absorb the spirit of the École; by the end of the century the major architectural schools in America had French professors of design who spread the gospel of the Beaux Arts. The World's Columbian Exposition of 1893, in Chicago, sealed the triumph of the Beaux Arts; most of the classical buildings of the exposition, dubbed the White City, came off the drawing boards of American architects who had been schooled in Paris.

The homes of many rich Americans were now designed to look like a Scottish castle, an English manor, a French château, an Italian palazzo, or a German burg. Even the houses of the middle class displayed a wealth of architectural ornament, inside and out, made of compo, a putty-like material painted to simulate decorative plasterwork or wood carving. Columns, pillars, capitals, friezes, masks, shields, moldings, and other ornaments were available in thousands of styles, patterns, and sizes.

Earlier Victorian houses in revival styles had been derived from romantic prints and bore only a symbolic resemblance to Old World models; they were the pleasant fruits of ignorance. The buildings of the Beaux Arts, or eclectic, period were historically "correct";* they were

---

* Correctness was aided by photography. Historic buildings had been recorded by photography since the 1840's, but there was no inexpensive way to publish photographic illustrations until 1880. The invention of the halftone process made it possible to reproduce architectural photographs in books and periodicals.

·Sketch·

·PINEAPPLE · HOUSE·
·SALEM · MASS·

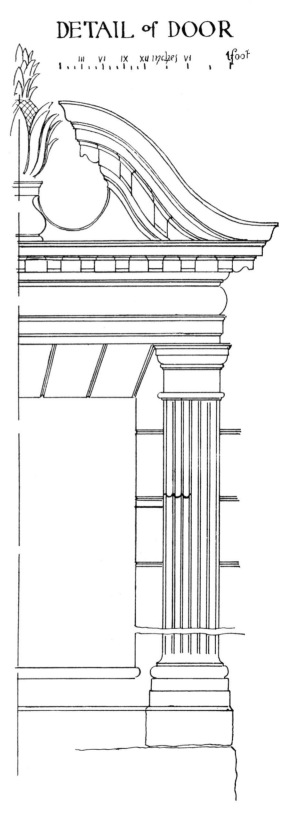

DETAIL of DOOR

III VI IX XII inches VI ₁foot

189

structurally sound, handsome, scholarly—sometimes too scholarly. Even Julien Guadet, the most famous professor at the École des Beaux Arts, wrote in 1902: "Archeology, which should be the handmaiden of the arts, can be their most formidable enemy. . . . All over the world, architecture has become bloodless by subordination to archeology."

The European Beaux Arts system also led to a revival of America's own architectural heritage. Architects who were already accustomed to study and sketch historic structures turned their attention to the buildings of eighteenth-century America. A typical drawing of 1887 is shown on page 189.

A few "Colonial" details, like the triple Palladian window and the swag or garland, had occasionally appeared on houses of the 1870's and 1880's, but the Colonial, or Georgian, Revival is a movement of the nineties. At first it was a style for a sophisticated minority in the East. Throughout the nineties most houses were still being built along complicated Queen Anne lines, but by the end of the century the simpler Colonial Revival style had worked its way down to the middle-class home.

Conventional histories of architecture give the entirely misleading impression that Victorianism was vanquished in the nineties by Frank Lloyd Wright and his followers.* In reality, "modern" architecture was a kind of underground movement in America until the middle of the twentieth century. "Modern" houses were built by the half dozen, "period" houses by the millions. Even today the typical suburban home is still superficially "Colonial" and a distant descendant of seventeenth-century palace architecture. The front lawn, front walk, and back yard are the court of honor and park of Versailles. Cement vases, lions, or Mexican and burro are the dwarfish heirs of Baroque sculpture, proclaiming, "My home is my palace."

This design for living was set at the turn of the twentieth century. Almost every new house was connected to water and sewer pipes and was wired for electric light and telephone. The railroad network was complete from coast to coast, the automobile was on the road, the airplane was three years away.

The present had arrived.

---

* The work of Frank Lloyd Wright and the "Prairie style" of the nineties are not discussed in this book, though they did not make a complete break with the traditional Victorian house.

Benjamin Barton Comegys, a Philadelphia banker, photographed in his library in about 1900. Surrounded by European artifacts, he exemplifies the cultural ambitions of the nineties. The house has been razed, but his paneled library is now installed in the Museum of History and Technology in Washington, D. C.

Richard Morris Hunt, the first American to graduate from the École des Beaux Arts in Paris, became architect to the Vanderbilt family, whose members shared a mania for extravagant houses. Biltmore, near Asheville, North Carolina, was commissioned in 1890 by George W. Vanderbilt, a twenty-six-year-old bachelor. It is in the style of a French Renaissance château; the estate covered 146,000 acres.

Two years later Hunt designed The Breakers, the summer "cottage" of George's brother, Cornelius Vanderbilt, at Newport, Rhode Island. It is patterned after the palaces of Genoa. The château in the middle distance is Ochre Court, the home of Ogden Goelet, also by Hunt; it is now a college for women. Between these two palaces is Vinland, a large house of the eighties.

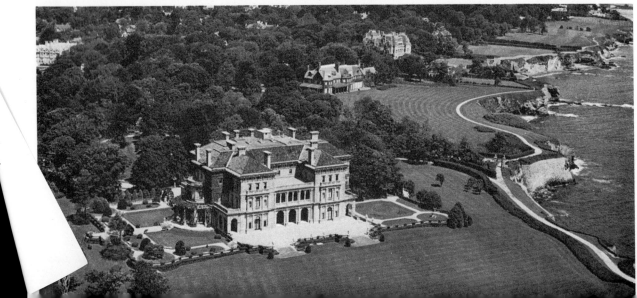

Horace Trumbauer, of Philadelphia, who never attended architectural school, became a specialist in designing homes for the very rich. This is Lynnewood Hall, at Elkins Park, Pennsylvania, of the 1890's, the home of Peter A. B. Widener, a streetcar magnate and art-collector who had begun his working life as a butcher's boy. It is much larger than the White House, though smaller than Buckingham Palace. The planner Jacques Gréber came from Paris to design the formal gardens. Lynnewood Hall now houses a seminary.

The overwhelming formality of these palaces is captured in a 1903 drawing by Charles Dana Gibson. The caption reads, "A castle in the air. These young girls who marry old millionaires should stop dreaming."

Meadow Lodge, at Bryn Mawr, Pennsylvania, seen here in a 1902 photograph. "The exquisitely picturesque" home of the dry-goods merchant Robert E. Strawbridge is in the half-timbered English style. This type of house became even more popular in affluent twentieth-century suburbs; it has been called Stockbrokers' Tudor.

The home of Frederick Pabst, German-born Milwaukee brewer, designed by George B. Ferry in the Renaissance style of Flanders in 1892. The columns of the former conservatory, in the right background, are embellished with carvings of barley and hops. The house is now the residence of the Roman Catholic archbishop of Milwaukee.

A Philadelphia row house from the 1890's pretending to
be a palace. Note that it is about the same size as its
plain neighbor.

Lindenwold, the home of Dr. Richard Vanselous Mattison, a chemical manufacturer, of Ambler, Pennsylvania. Lindenwold stands in a walled park with gates, towers, lake, and bridge; it is now a home for children, recalling a description of a foundling asylum, written by Thorstein Veblen: "An edifice faced with some aesthetically objectionable but expensive stone, covered with grotesque and incongruous details, and designed, in its battlemented walls and turrets and its massive portals and strategic approaches, to suggest certain barbaric methods of warfare."

Like a benevolent feudal lord, Dr. Mattison built a street of castlelike houses, no two alike, for the executives of his company in the nineties.

The coach house of one of the Mattison company homes, with its towers and shingled gable, is patterned after a medieval German city gate.

Roslyn, at Lancaster, Pennsylvania, the home of Peter
T. Watt, a penniless immigrant from the Orkney Islands
who had become a successful dry-goods merchant, was
ready for his family of eight on his wife's birthday in
1896. The architect Emlen Urban designed the house in
"Baronial" style to recall the owner's native Scotland.

The core of Roslyn is a high hall with open staircase and elaborate woodwork; a pulpitlike landing on the stairs is lighted by a great window of leaded glass. On the mantelpiece is the Scots version of a popular Victorian sentiment, "EAST WEST HAME'S BEST."

An English Georgian mansion of 1899, in red brick, trimmed with light-blue marble, was the home of William H. Shelmerdine, a Philadelphia cement-manufacturer. It now houses a firm of architects.

In the sixties many Colonial- and Federal-style houses had been "Victorianized" by adding a mansard roof. Around the turn of the century some Victorian homes were "Colonialized." This is the remodeled facade of Villa Fontana, the home of the famous cartoonist Thomas Nast, at Morristown, New Jersey.

A typical page from a catalog of architectural ornament

Colonial Revival houses are sometimes not easy to tell from Colonial buildings. On Brattle Street, in Cambridge, Massachusetts, is the famous house that served as Washington's headquarters in 1776 and was the home of Henry Wadsworth Longfellow for forty-five years. Four doors away stands this Colonial Revival house, built in 1887 for the poet's daughter Annie Longfellow Thorp and designed by his nephew, the architect Alexander Wadsworth Longfellow, Jr.

The home of William T. Davis, a historian, at Plymouth, Massachusetts, photographed in about 1900, was described by his grandson, the historian Henry-Russell Hitchcock:

We lived in a Neo-Colonial house built for him in the 1890's by Joseph Everett Chandler, a Boston architect of Plymouth origin who was one of the earliest authorities on the Colonial. ... The plan, though compact and rectangular, includes a large stair hall that is a real room, opening by a wide pair of doors—never closed —into the "parlor" or living room, which opens similarly into the dining room. The plan has practically as much spatial flow as Wright's earliest houses of the same years; and like them it is in the continuing tradition of the Shingle Style—indeed, the exterior is shingled, except for the white-painted "Colonial" trim, and had a piazza all the way across the front in an earlier nineteenth-century tradition.

A turn-of-the-century interior, with two characteristic pieces of furniture: the adjustable Morris chair and the Colonial Revival Windsor rocker

John Calvin Stevens, of Portland, Maine, was one of the first architects to revive the Colonial style. He designed these homes in the 1880's for the employees of a paper mill and wrote: "Homelike cottages have been built, and a system of rents and payments established which encourages the operatives to acquire and control their own homesteads. . . . A feature of summertime here is the rich bloom of flowers about the pretty cottages. . . . Here is an example suggesting the solution of certain social problems. In all the history of Cumberland Mills there is no record of a strike." The Cumberland paper mill of the S. D. Warren Company and these houses are now part of Westbrook, Maine.

A Street in Cumberland Mills.   J.C.S.

In 1889 the twenty-six-year-old owner of a small saw-
mill in Michigan built this home with his own hands; it
is the trim work of a man who had taught himself to
repair watches when he was a boy of twelve. Two years
later, he left his "square house" to take a city job, tend-
ing steam engines at the Edison Company. His name was
Henry Ford.

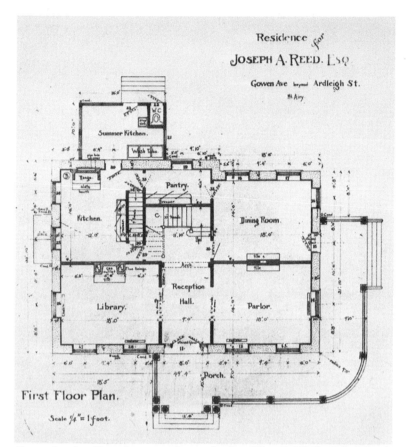

Residence for
JOSEPH A. REED. ESQ

Gowen Ave beyond Ardleigh St.
Mt. Airy.

Summer Kitchen.

Wash Tubs

Pantry.

Kitchen.

Dining Room.

Reception Hall.

Library.

Parlor.

Porch.

First Floor Plan.

Scale ¼" = 1 foot.

Joseph A. Reed was elected sheriff of Philadelphia in 1898, the year after he moved to this fieldstone house, designed by George T. Pearson. The "center hall plan" marks a return to Colonial tradition.

Behind the oval window on the second floor is a small study, a good room in which to close the door on the children and write a book. You are now reading the book.

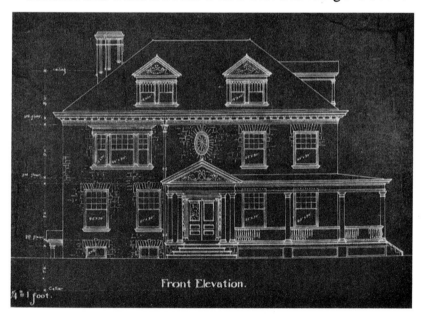

Front Elevation.

¼" = 1 foot.

205

APPENDIX I

AN INCOMPLETE GUIDE
TO AMERICAN VICTORIANA

The key word in the title of this appendix is "incomplete." Throughout the world more houses were built during the nineteenth century than in all previous ages combined. In America the student of Victorian architecture has a wide range to explore. There are over thirty-five thousand municipalities and townships in the United States, and most communities have some buildings that survive from the Victorian period. This brief list is therefore only a sampling of some neighborhoods and houses which have come to my attention. County seats, of which there are over three thousand, are usually good places to visit, with the homes and offices of affluent lawyers near the courthouse square.

I have made no distinction here between private homes and public places. Sightseers should respect the privacy of the former. The museums and historical societies listed here are in Victorian houses, or they display collections of the period; there are many more. Check with local tourist agencies or chambers of commerce for more information and for details on admission.

Alabama

Courtland. Rocky Hill Castle, a villa of c. 1850

Marion. Carlisle Hall, an Italianate villa

Mobile. The city is noted for many houses with ornamental ironwork, especially in the East Church Street and DeTonti Square historic districts.

Tuscaloosa. Cherokee, an Italianate mansion

Alaska

Sitka. The old Russian capital of Alaska has a number of wooden Victorian houses.

Arizona

Phoenix. Pioneer Arizona Foundation's Pioneer Village

Prescott. Old Governor's Mansion (1864)

Tombstone. Pioneer Home Museum

Tucson. Several houses in which Victorian styles are executed in the local adobe (sun-dried brick) material

Arkansas

Hot Springs. Wildwood, elaborate house of 1884

Little Rock. The Quapaw Quarter of the city has notable buildings, including the houses of Governor Augustus Garland (1873) and of Dr. Charles J. Lincoln (1872).

California

Arcadia. Lucky Baldwin estate, now the Arboretum (see page 162)

Belmont. The Ralston Mansion (see page 82)

Chico. Bidwell Mansion

Columbia. Old mining town, Historic State Park

Eureka. Lumber port with outstanding Victorian business blocks and houses (see pages 164–166)

Los Angeles. Some Victorian neighborhoods remain in this modern metropolis, including MacArthur Park and Adams Boulevard. Angelino Heights is a neighborhood of Queen Anne houses. Heritage Square is being developed as an outdoor museum with nineteenth-century buildings. (See pages 131 and 160.)

Martinez. The ranch and house of the naturalist John Muir

Nevada City. Former gold-mining town with fine houses

Oakland. The Oakland Museum has good Victorian displays.

Palm Springs. Desert Museum

Redlands. Hermosa Vista (see page 161)

Sacramento. Lavish houses of the sixties and seventies include the former Governor's Mansion, the E. B. Crocker House and Art Gallery, and the Leland Stanford Mansion.

St. Helena. The Rhine House, a wine-growers home of 1883

San Diego. Villa Montezuma, the ornate house of the musician and author Jesse Shepard

San Francisco. No large American city has more fascinating Victorian blocks and homes. Neighborhoods with distinctive wooden houses (see page 95) are Pacific Heights, Russian Hill, Mission, Twin Peaks. Houses include the Flood Mansion, on Nob Hill, and the California Historical Society, in the Whittier Mansion.

San Joaquin. Pioneer Museum

San Jose. Winchester Mystery House, the home of an eccentric woman, was under construction for thirty-eight years.

San Rafael. Ira Cook House in Boyd Park

Santa Barbara. Fernald House (1862)

Tiburon. The Lyford House, now the Audubon Society

Colorado

Aspen. Former silver-mining town, now resort, with many Victorian houses

Black Hawk. The Lace House, a former parsonage, with gingerbread trim

Colorado Springs. The Pioneers Museum; the Major McAllister House of 1873

Denver. Once known as the City of Mansions. Many massive houses of cattle and mining barons still stand in the Capitol Hill section (including the houses of Richard B. Pearce, Donald Fletcher, Dennis Sheedy, James J. Brown, Governor Evans, Thomas B. Croke). The Richthofen and Kittredge mansions are in the Montclair section.

Georgetown. The Hamill House of 1867; the colorful Frank Maxwell House of c. 1890

Greeley. The Meeker Museum

Leadville. The Healy House of 1878 is now a museum

Pueblo. Rosemount, the Thatcher Mansion of 1891; now a museum

Trinidad. The Bloom Mansion in the Second Empire style, now a museum

Connecticut

Bridgeport. P. T. Barnum Museum

Groton. Monument House

Hartford. Armsmear, the mansion of Samuel Colt (1857), is now a home for retired ministers. In the Nook Farm section are three neighboring houses of the greatest architectural and historic interest: the Mark Twain Home, the Harriet Beecher Stowe Home, and the Stowe-Day Research Library in the Day House (see pages 148–149).

Middletown. Several outstanding houses are now buildings of Wesleyan University.

Mystic. Mystic Seaport Marine Association, an outdoor museum

New Haven. Hillhouse Avenue is a noted street of fine residences. The Davies House, on Prospect Street (1867), is now the Culinary Institute of America.

New London. Lyman Allen Museum

Newtown. Attractive main street

Norwalk. Lockwood-Mathews Mansion (see pages 114–115)

Norwich. Broadway is a street with a variety of impressive houses.

Portland. The unusual sight of two neighboring octagons

Watertown. Small town with variety of homes

Woodstock. Roseland (see page 48)

Delaware

Dover. North State Street in this small state capital is lined with fine houses.

Seaford. The Italianate Governor Ross House

Wilmington. Delaware Avenue has mansions and town houses c. 1850–1880.

Winterthur. The period rooms of the Henry Francis du Pont Museum are pre-Victorian, but the museum is now also a center of Victorian studies.

District of Columbia

No other large American city surpasses Washington in number, quality, and variety of Victorian buildings. Both the North West and South East (Capitol Hill) sections have dozens of blocks of large and small row houses; pastel colors and bay-windowed facades are characteristic of Washington. Georgetown is an elegant neighborhood of town houses and a few detached villas. Logan Square is a circle with an equestrian monument, surrounded by colorful mansarded houses. The Columbia Historical Society, in the Heurich Mansion of 1894, has interesting furnishings. The Smithsonian Institution's Museum of History and Technology displays several period rooms and collections of Victoriana. (See pages 86 and 172.)

Florida

Key West. A subtropical resort of attractive wooden houses with verandas

St. Augustine. The Villa Zorayda, an unusual Moorish house of 1883

Georgia

Athens. Handsome university town with Greek Revival and Early Victorian homes; fine ironwork; the Mell House (1848)

Atlanta. Wren's Nest, the home of the author Joel Chandler Harris (1880)

Macon. The Hay House, Italianate mansion of 1855

Madison. Boxwood, an elegant house of 1855

Savannah. The historic area with its twenty-four tree-shaded squares, is one of America's most beautiful townscapes. There are many Victorian houses near Monterey Square, Madison Square, and Forsythe Park. Other houses include the Italianate Dube House and the Gothic Revival Green-Meldrim House (see page 41).

Valdosta. The Crescent, Classic Revival house of 1898

Washington. Washington-Wilkes Historical Museum (see page 56)

Hawaii

Honolulu. King Kamehameha's fanciful wooden cottage in the Monalua Garden; late Victorian towered villas on the slopes above downtown

Idaho

Aurora. Historical Museum in Tanner House

Boise. Governor Moses Alexander House (1890's); C. W. Moore House (1891)

Moscow. Governor McConnell House

Illinois

Aledo. Mercer County Museum

Aurora. Historical Museum in Tanner House of 1856

Bloomington. David Davis House, now a museum

Cairo. River port with handsome houses: Riverlore (1865); Magnolia Manor (1869)

Chicago. Victorian residential neighborhoods include Old Town Triangle, Fullerton Avenue, Alta Vista. Houses include the Swedish Engineers Club, in a baroque mansion and the Nickerson House (see page 174). The Glessner House, by Richardson, is now an architectural foundation. The former model industrial city of Pullman (1880's) is now within Chicago.

Decatur. Art Center in Millikin House of 1876

Evanston. Historical Society in Dawes House of 1894; Frances Willard House (1865)

Galena. River town with many Victorian buildings: the U. S. Grant House, presented to the general in 1865; Belvedere, a villa of 1857

Oak Park. A comfortable late-nineteenth-century suburb with the first home and studio of Frank Lloyd Wright (1889) and the Queen Anne house in which Ernest Hemingway was born

Quincy. Quincy Historical Society Museum; Bull House (1850); Huffman House (1885)

Rockford. Erlander House Museum

Springfield. The Executive Mansion; the Lincoln House, where he lived from 1844 to 1861; Edwards Place, now the Art Association

Indiana

Aurora. Hillforest, a mansion of 1852, slightly reminiscent of riverboat design

Geneva. Limberlost Cabin, home of the author Gene Stratton Porter (1895)

Indianapolis. The Lockerbie Square neighborhood, including the house of the poet James Whitcomb Riley; many mansions on Delaware Street, including the home of President Benjamin Harrison (1874); the Morris-Butler Mansion, now a museum of decorative arts

Lafayette. The Tippecanoe County Historical Association in the Gothic Revival Fowler House

New Albany. A variety of Italianate and Second Empire houses

New Castle. Henry County Historical Society

New Harmony. Former Utopian community with the Gothic house of the reformer Dr. David Dale Owen (1859)

Rushville. Rush County Historical Society

South Bend. The Richardsonian Studebaker House

Iowa

Amana. Utopian community, established in the 1850's

Cedar Falls. Cedar Falls Historical Society

Clermont. Governor Larrabee House

Council Bluffs. Grenville M. Dodge House (1869)

Des Moines. Terrace Hill, the towering mansion of the banker B. F. Allen (1869); the Hoyt Sherman Place (1877)

Dubuque. Dubuque County Historical Society (Ham House Museum)

Marshalltown. Marshall County Historical Society (Sower House)

Mount Pleasant. Harlan-Lincoln House, the home of Lincoln's son

Oskaloosa. Mahaska County Historical Society.

Sioux City. Peirce Mansion, now a museum

Waterloo. Rensselaer Russell House

Kansas

Athol. "Home on the Range Cabin" (Higley House) of 1872

Baldwin. Old Cattle Museum

Carlyle. General Frederick Funston House (1860)

Ellsworth. Historical Society Museum in Hogden House of 1875

Hillsboro. Adobe Pioneer House

Lawrence. An unusual variety of fine houses, including the Italianate Riggs and Thacher homes

Newton. Warkentin House, home of Mennonite settler

Kentucky

Lexington. In and near the city are a number of notable villas, including the Gothic Revival houses Ingleside and Aylesford, and the Italianate Glengarry. Ashland, the home of Henry Clay, was rebuilt as an Italianate house in 1857; it has outstanding furnishings.

Louisiana

New Orleans. The distinctive residential architecture of the city in the French tradition was built until well into the Victorian period. Largest concentration of ornamental cast-iron work in America. In the Garden district are many houses of Victorian design or details; they include the Briggs-Staub, Short-Moran, Koch-Mays, and Musson-Bell houses. The Gallier House, home of the nineteenth-century architect, is now a museum.

Reserve. San Francisco Plantation, in "Steamboat Gothic" style (1849)

St. Francisville. Afton Villa, rare example of Gothic Revival plantation house

Terrebone Parish. Ardoyne Plantation, fanciful wooden house of 1894

Maine

Augusta. James G. Blaine House; home and furnishings of the statesman

Bangor. Many fine wooden houses

Kennebunk. The Wedding Cake House, with elaborate wooden trim

Portland. Victoria Mansion (Morse House) of 1859, a lavish Italianate villa

Maryland

Baltimore. A city noted for its town houses. Mount Vernon Place, with brownstone homes and public buildings, is one of the handsomest cityscapes in America. The development of the American row house from 1830 to 1940 can be seen in chronological order by walking north on St. Paul Street. The Maryland Historical Society is in the former Pratt House. Evergreen, the Garrett mansion, is now a rare-book library. Clifton, an Italianate villa, is in Clifton Park. Roland Park was one of America's first planned garden suburbs (1892).

Bel Air. Attractive houses on tree-shaded main street.

Frederick. County seat with fine courthouse square

Glen Echo. The Clara Barton House

Westminster. Carroll County Farm Museum

Massachusetts

Boston. Changing styles of town houses from 1860 to 1900 can be seen by walking west on Commonwealth Avenue from Arlington Street, crossing the alphabetically named Berkeley, Clarendon, Dartmouth, Exeter, Fairfield, Gloucester, and Hereford Streets (see page 133). The Gibson House, now a museum. The Museum of Fine Arts collections.

Cambridge. Almost every type of Victorian house is represented on the winding streets of this university city (see pages 43, 181, and 201).

Cheshire. The mansarded Eugene Bowen House

Eastham. The Penniman House (see page 123)

Fall River. Rock Street; Fall River Historical Society, in an impressive granite mansion (which was moved over a mile in 1870!)

Gloucester. The stone house of the painter Fitz Hugh Lane

Groton. Historical Society in Boutwell House

Lenox. Fashionable Berkshire Hills resort with large summer homes of the eighties and nineties

Lowell. Many fine mansions and houses

Milford. Good variety of Victorian houses

New Bedford. The Union Street neighborhood

Oak Bluffs. Colorful Camp Meeting cottages (see page 58); other summer cottages with fanciful woodwork (see page 154)

Rockport. Sandy Bay Historical Society and Museum

Salem. The Essex Institute

Swampscott. Large shingled summer houses

Worcester. Art Museum

Michigan

Dearborn. The collections of Americana established by Henry Ford are unsurpassed. The vast Henry Ford Museum exhibits Victorian furnishings and many other nineteenth-century objects. Greenfield Village is an outdoor museum with many buildings of historic inter-est, including the homes and workshops of famous Americans, brought here and reerected.

Fayette. Fayette State Park Historic Site

Grand Rapids. Products of this famous furniture-manufacturing city are displayed in the Public Museum.

Grosse Ile. Some outstanding Gothic Revival villas

Ionia. The Hall-Fowler Library in an Italianate Mansion of 1870

Lansing. Michigan Historical Commission Museum

Manchester. Several villas of the fifties

Marshall. The Gothic Revival Abner Baker House; the Italianate Joy-Benedict House; the Abner Pratt House, or "Honolulu House," of 1860, now a museum

Midland. Midland County Historical Association

Muskegon. Hackley House of 1889

Port Sanilac. Sanilac County Historical Society in Loop Mansion

Washington. The Andrus Octagon of 1860

Minnesota

Faribault. Alexander Faribault House (1853)

Hastings. The General William G. LeDuc House (1866)

Hudson. Moffat Octagon of 1855

Mankato. Blue Earth County Historical Society in Hubbard House

Morton. Renville County Historical Society Museum

New Ulm. Stone and brick houses in German settlement of sixties and seventies

St. Paul. The Ramsey House (see page 122) and the Gibbs House are now museums of the Ramsey County Historical Society. The James J. Hill House is the red sandstone mansion of the financier (1889).

Sauk Centre. Boyhood home of Sinclair Lewis

Winona. Henry D. Huff House (1857)

Mississippi

Columbus. Several fine mansions

Holly Springs. Outstanding Victorian houses include Cedarhurst, The Magnolias, and Walter Place.

Natchez. Longwood (see pages 104–105)

Vicksburg. Cedar Grove

Missouri

Affton. The Benoist House, an Italianate villa

Festus. Nearby is Selma Hall, a towering villa overlooking the Mississippi.

Hannibal. Mark Twain Boyhood Home and Museum

Independence. Home of Harry S Truman (Gates-Wallace House of 1865)

Jefferson City. The Governor's Mansion (1871); Cole County Historical Society Museum in former Governor Brown House

Keytesville. The Redding-Hill House

Laclede. General Pershing Boyhood Home (1860)

Lamar. The house in which Harry S Truman was born

Mexico. Audrain County Historical Society Museum

St. Joseph. St. Joseph Museum in Gothic Revival Wyeth House

St. Louis. A city of row houses with distinctive galleries. Houses include Henry Shaw's country house, Tower Grove, and his town house in Botanical Garden. The Campbell House is now a museum. In the West End are several residential "places," private streets with elaborate gates, of the nineties. The James R. Clemens House with iron columns is now a missionary society.

Montana

Butte. The Copper King Mansion

Helena. Montana Historical Society; the Chessman House (former governor's mansion)

Virginia City. Old gold-mining town, the best known of Montana's many ghost towns.

White Sulphur Springs. The Stone Castle (1890's)

Nebraska

Brownsville. John L. Carson House (1860)

Lincoln. Fairview, the home of William Jennings Bryan

North Platte. Scout's Rest, the home of Buffalo Bill

Red Cloud. The Willa Cather House

Nevada

Reno. Between Reno and Carson City is the Bowers Mansion, with lavish furnishings of the silver-boom era.

Virginia City. Former silver-mining town with outstanding Victorian public buildings and houses

New Hampshire

Concord. President Franklin Pierce's house

Madison. Historical Society in house of 1885

Manchester. Variety of Victorian homes, including several octagons

New Jersey

Belvidere. County seat with fine courthouse square

Bordentown. Riverside houses

Caldwell. The manse in which Grover Cleveland was born

Camden. Walt Whitman's small house

Cape May. This old ocean resort might be called America's capital of gingerbread architecture (see page 55).

Cranbury. Colonial, Victorian, and Colonial Revival homes on village main street

Edgewater Park. Estates facing river (see pages 124 and 150)

Flemington. Handsome houses line Main Street (see pages 126 and 155).

Freehold. Another county seat with attractive Main Street (see pages 54 and 80)

Glassboro. Hollybush, villa on State College campus

Hopewell. Hopewell Museum

Long Branch. This seashore town and the neighboring resorts of Elberon and Deal have many impressive summer homes of the eighties and nineties.

Morristown. Macculloch Avenue; Acorn Hall (see pages 70–71); Villa Fontana (see page 200)

Newark. Town houses; New Jersey Historical Society

Newton. The Merriam House (see page 150)

Palermo. The colorful Captain Sylvanus Corson house

Princeton. Handsome university town with many types of nineteenth-century houses well represented; Prospect, the Italianate residence of Princeton University's president

South Seaville. Camp Meeting cottages

West Orange. Glenmont, the home of Thomas Edison

New Mexico

El Rito. Small mercantile town with distinctive houses

Las Vegas. Fifth, Sixth, and Seventh streets have bracketed, mansard, and Queen Anne houses.

Santa Fe. Specimens of most nineteenth-century styles on Palace Avenue; the Preston House

Springer. The Mills House, Second Empire style in adobe construction

New York

Alexandria Bay. The turn-of-the-century Boldt's Castle on an island

Auburn. The house and furnishings of the statesman William H. Seward

Bethpage. Old Bethpage Restoration, outdoor museum

Buffalo. Some mansions remain on Delaware Avenue, once known as Millionaires' Row (see page 85).

Cazenovia. Small town with variety of Victorian homes; the town hall is in a Gothic cottage

Centerport. William K. Vanderbilt Museum

Chautauqua. Lakeside cottages at the educational Chautauqua Institution

Childs. Cobblestone Society

Cooperstown. New York State Historical Association; Farmer's Museum

Elmira. Arnot Art Gallery; Mark Twain's garden house study

Garden City. Planned residential community, established in the seventies

Geneva. Fine lakeside Main Street with attractive houses; the Moore Octagon, with cast-iron verandas

Georgetown. The Timothy Brown House (see page 59)

Hudson. Nearby is Olana (see pages 106–107).

Hyde Park. The Franklin D. Roosevelt Home; the Frederick Vanderbilt Mansion (1896)

Irvington. Elaborate domed octagon

Jamestown. The Governor Fenton House

Kinderhook. Lindenwold, the home of Martin Van Buren

Monroe. Old Museum Village of Smith's Clove

New York City. In Manhattan there are early- and mid-Victorian town houses in the Greenwich Village, Washington Square, Gramercy Park, and Chelsea areas. In the Murray Hill section some Victorian carriage houses have been converted into homes. The Theodore Roosevelt birthplace is in that area. Larger, eclectic residences of the late nineteenth century are on Fifth Avenue, facing Central Park, and on the fashionable Upper East Side; many have been converted to institutional use. In this area are the Metropolitan Museum of Art and the Museum of the City of New York. Many interesting Victorian houses are off the Manhattan tourist track. Brooklyn Heights is an elegant neighborhood of brownstone houses (see page 92). Clinton Hill, Cobble Hill, Bedford-Stuyvesant, are other row-house neighborhoods of Brooklyn. Park Slope has a variety of Queen Anne and Richardsonian town houses and mansions. Prospect Park South and Flushing have late-Victorian detached homes. The Litchfield House is in Prospect Park. The Brooklyn Museum displays period rooms. In the Bronx there is Font Hill (see page 36). Staten Island has many types of Victorian houses, including some in surprisingly rural settings.

Oneida. Utopian community established in 1848

Owego. Good houses near attractive courthouse square

Oyster Bay. Sagamore Hill, the home of Theodore Roosevelt (see page 177)

Pittsford. Fine Main Street

Poughkeepsie. In the historic district, between Franklin and Montgomery streets, are large and handsome mansarded and towered houses. Springside was the country estate of Matthew Vassar. Nearby is Locust Grove, the home of Samuel Morse.

Rhinebeck. Hudson Valley village with attractive houses (see page 119)

Rochester. Variety of Victorian houses in the Third Ward; Woodside (Rochester Historical Society); the Barry House (see page 72). Rochester is the center of the cobblestone-house region.

Saratoga Springs. Famous resort with High Victorian villas

Sea Cliff. Summer homes of the eighties and nineties

Shinnecock. Home and studio of William Merritt Chase (see page 178)

Southampton. Many fine summer homes

Staatsburg. The Ogden Mills Mansion

Tarrytown. Lyndhurst (see pages 38–39); Sunnyside, the home of Washington Irving; Historical Society of the Tarrytowns

Troy. Fine brick and brownstone town houses

Tuxedo Park. Fashionable planned community of the eighties (see page 179)

Utica. Fountain Elms, an Italianate villa of 1850, now a museum

Warwick. Attractive Main Street

Watkins Glen. Yorker Yankee Village Museum

Wellsville. The Pink House (see page 78)

Westfield. Good villas and cottages; Chautauqua County Historical Society

Yonkers. The Hudson River Museum in the Trevor Mansion of 1876, well related to new buildings

North Carolina

Asheville. Biltmore (see page 192)

Greensboro. Blandwood, Italianate villa of 1844

Kernersville. Korner's Folly, mansion of 1880

Raleigh. On North Blount Street are the Heck-Andrews and Hinsdale houses of the seventies.

The Governor's Mansion of 1891 is in the Queen Anne manner.

Wilmington. Italianate villas between Second and Fifth streets; Bellamy Mansion (see page 81)

North Dakota

Bismarck. Governor's Mansion (Fisher House) of 1884

Medora. Château de Mores, now a museum

Ohio

Cincinnati. The John Hauck House and other town houses on Dayton Street; the Taft House (1850); the Pendleton House (1870). Clifton is a good example of an elegant Victorian suburb.

Dayton. The home of the poet Paul Laurence Dunbar

Fremont. Spiegel Grove, the home of President Rutherford B. Hayes

Gambier. College town with Gothic Revival houses

Gibraltar Island. Lake Erie summer home of financier Jay Cooke, now part of State Ecology laboratory

Marion. The house of President Warren Harding

Mentor. Lawnfield, the home of President Garfield; the Gothic Bolton House

Oxford. Oxford Museum Association

Wellington. Good assemblage of Victorian homes

West Liberty. The Piatt Castles

Zanesville. Art Institute in former Bailey House

Oklahoma

Kingfisher. Shingled Governor Seay House

Marietta. Bill Washington House; home of cattleman (1887)

Oklahoma City. Fifteenth Street has turn-of-the-century mansions.

Oregon

Astoria. Clatsop County Historical Society in Flavel House of 1887

Brownsville. Linn County Historical Society in former Moyer House

Jacksonville. Southern Oregon Historical Museum

Portland. Surviving houses of the eighties and nineties include "Piggott's Folly" on Buckingham Terrace, and the Nicholas-Lang, Capt. John Brown, Mackenzie, and Bickel houses.

Salem. Salem Art Association in Bush House of 1887; Port-Bingham House

Pennsylvania

Ambler. The Mattison houses (see pages 196–197)

Doylestown. County seat with attractive houses: the Mercer Museum; the James Loran Memorial House

Ephrata. The Connell House, now a museum

Glenside. Grey Towers, a castle of the nineties, on the campus of Beaver College

Greensburg. Westmoreland County Art Museum

Jim Thorpe. The mansion of the coal millionaire Asa Packer

Lancaster. Center of the Pennsylvania Dutch country with characteristic red brick houses, painted brick red. East Orange Street is a fine townscape. Wheatland was the home of President James Buchanan.

Landis Valley. Pennsylvania Farm Museum

Marietta. Riverview Tower (see page 124)

Montrose. Attractive county seat

Philadelphia. A city of row houses; good examples in Center City, west of Broad Street. Woodland Terrace in West Philadelphia is a fine block of Italianate villas. Germantown and Chestnut Hill have many distinctive fieldstone houses. The Ebenezer Maxwell Mansion in Germantown is being developed as a Victorian museum. The Woodmere Gallery; Burholme (see pages 90–91). Victoriana in the Philadelphia Museum of Art. Great variety of late-nineteenth-century houses in the Main Line suburbs.

Pittsburgh. Victorian residential neighborhoods include Shadyside, the Mexican War streets, Manchester, the Lincoln-Beech Avenue area. In suburban Wilkinsburg is the ornate Singer

Mansion of 1865. Evergreen Hamlet is an outstanding planned community of Gothic cottages (1850's).

West Chester. Handsome county seat with houses of red brick and of a distinctive local green stone; Chester County Historical Society

Rhode Island

Narragansett. Late-nineteenth-century seaside cottages

Newport. No American city of any size surpasses this fashionable resort in the variety and quality of Victorian residences of every style built between 1840 and 1900. The Breakers, Marble House, Château-sur-Mer, Belcourt Castle, and The Elms are lavish mansions that are now open to the public. (See pages 40, 116–117, 128, 159, 177, and 192.)

Providence. The College Hill section has fine Victorian and Colonial Revival houses.

South Carolina

Charleston. City of famous Georgian architecture also has houses of Victorian design and details: the Middleton House and Gallery; the Rodgers Mansion

Dillon. The James W. Dillon House

Greenville. The Captain Norwood House, colorful mansion of 1876

Rambert. Nearby is Millvale Plantation, with main house of 1890, old mill, and lake.

Union. Governor Jeter House (1859)

South Dakota

Deadwood. Old gold-mining town

Hot Springs. A Victorian spa

Lead. Old gold-mining town

Watertown. The Governor Mellette House of 1883

Tennessee

Chattanooga. Houston Memorial Antiques Museum

Jackson. Casey Jones House (1880)

Jonesboro. Good collection of Victorian homes

Memphis. Four outstanding towered mansions (Annandale, Lee House, Fontaine House, Mallory House) are open to the public and form a "Victorian Village."

Nashville. Nearby is Belle Meade, a mansion of 1853, with opulent Victorian furnishings.

Rugby. House and School of Thomas Hughes, British Victorian author

Texas

Austin. The Major Littlefield House of 1883

Bonham. The Brownlee House; the Scarborough House

Calvert. Good Queen Anne houses

Decatur. The Waggoner House of 1884

Fulton Beach. Mansard mansion of George W. Fulton (1872)

Galveston. A city of fantastic Victorian houses, many designed by the local architect Nicholas J. Clayton. The Gresham House of 1888, later known as the Bishop's Palace; the Trube House (see page 169); the Sonnentheil House (see page 157).

Jefferson. "The House of Seasons," with spiral staircase and cupola with colored glass

Nacogdoches. Ashford Jones House

Palestine. Queen Anne houses

Paris. General Sam Bell Maxey House

San Antonio. San Antonio Conservation Society in Steves House of 1876; Ike West House

Victoria. Museum Association in McNamara House of 1869

Utah

Midway. The Watkins House (see page 49)

Salt Lake City. Brigham Young's home, the Beehive House, with Victorian furnishings; the Utah Historical Society in the former Kearns Mansion

Vermont

Montpelier. Attractive small state capital

North Bennington. Governor McCullough Mansion

Plymouth. The Calvin Coolidge Homestead (1876)

Proctor. Wilson's Castle (1867)

Shelburne. The Shelburne Museum has many nineteenth-century buildings and outstanding collections of Victoriana.

Strafford. The Justin Smith Morrill Homestead, a Gothic Revival villa of 1848

Virginia

Alexandria. Red brick town houses

Orange. Nearby is Mayhurst, an Italianate villa of 1859.

Port Royal. Nearby is Camden (see pages 68–69).

Richmond. A city of town houses and much ornamental ironwork. Houses include Morson's Row, a group of three bow-fronted town houses; the "White House of the Confederacy" (Brockenbough House); the Valentine Museum, with collections of Victoriana; the Haxall House, now a club.

Washington

Bellingham. The fanciful Gamwell House of 1892

Hoquiam. "The Castle" (Lytle House)

Port Townsend. A lumber town with colorful late Victorian houses (see page 163)

Puyallup. Meeker Mansion

Seattle. Queen Anne Hill, with some remaining houses of that style

Spokane. Large homes built during mining boom of the nineties; Eastern Washington State Historical Society

Vancouver. Elaborate wooden houses

Walla-Walla. The Governor Moore House and other homes with fine Queen Anne woodwork

West Virginia

Berkeley Springs. "The Castle" of 1887

Morgantown. Alexander Wade House of 1872

Wheeling. Historic Mansion House and Gallery in Oglebay Park

White Sulphur Springs. Famous nineteenth-century resort

Wisconsin

Elkhorn. Walworth County Historical Society

Fond du Lac. Galloway House Museum

Janesville. The Tallman House of 1857, now a museum

Hudson. St. Croix Valley Historical Society in Moffat octagon of 1865

Madison. Fine residential section near Lake Mendota with houses built of local buff stone. They include the Old Executive Mansion, the Italianate Pierce House, and the Second Empire Kendall and Keenan Houses.

Maple Bluff. The home of Robert M. LaFollette (1860)

Milwaukee. Once known as the Cream City for its buildings of cream-colored brick. Many Victorian houses remain. The Machek House is an unusual cottage of 1886, designed by an Austrian woodcarver. The towering Wisconsin Club was originally the Alexander Mitchell Mansion. Late Victorian mansions include the Baroque Kalvelage House, the Gothic Goodrich House, and the Pabst House (see page 194).

Oconto. Oconto County Historical Society Museum

Prairie du Chien. The Villa Louis (Dousman House) is now a museum.

Sauk City. Sauk-Prairie Historical Society

Superior. Douglas County Historical Society

Watertown. The large Richards octagon of 1853

Wyoming

Cheyenne. This cattle town was once known as the richest city of its size in the world. Some houses remain from this boom period of the eighties and nineties.

Canada

Bowmanville, Ontario. Bowmanville Museum

Brantford, Ontario. The Bell Homestead (see page 47)

Cardston, Alberta. Cardston Historical Society

Como, Quebec. Riverfront estates

Edmonton, Alberta. John Walter Historical Site

Hamilton, Ontario. Outstanding mansions include Italianate Dundurn Castle (1835) and Whitehern (1848), the Gothic Rock Castle (1848). Fine rows of town houses, called by the British term terraces.

Kingston, Ontario. Bellevue, or "Teacaddy Castle," home of Sir John A. Macdonald; Elizabeth Cottage

London, Ontario. Victoria House Museum

Lunenburg, Nova Scotia. Fishing town with delightful wooden houses

Montreal, Quebec. Interesting contrast between the French sections (rows of mansarded houses with distinctive high basements and front steps) and the English-style western suburbs. Ravenscrag is the Italianate mansion of Sir Hugh Allan.

Morrisburg, Ontario. Upper Canada village, outdoor museum

New Westminster, British Columbia. Irving House of 1862

Oshawa, Ontario. Henry House Museum

Ottawa, Ontario. Outstanding Victorian public buildings and fine residential sections

Toronto, Ontario. Fine terraces; Mackenzie House, home of early mayor; Sherbourne House; the Gothic Oakham House

Victoria, British Columbia. Art Gallery in Spencer Mansion; Helmcken House; Craigdarroch Castle of 1889; the Maltwood Museum of the Arts and Crafts Movement

Windsor, Ontario. Halliburton Memorial Museum

Winnipeg, Manitoba. Ross House (1852).

APPENDIX II

YOU ARE NOT ALONE

Many organizations share your interest in the study and preservation of ninteenth-century architecture.

Government Agencies

Two agencies of the Federal Government are concerned with these matters:

The Historic American Buildings Survey, in Washington, a branch of the U.S. National Park Service, was established in 1933. HABS has recorded many thousands of structures by measured drawings, photographs, and written documentation. It has one of the largest such collections in the world.

The National Register of Historic Places, in Washington, is also under the U.S. National Park Service. It has liaison officers in every state and designates National Historic Landmarks.

All states have similar official agencies under various names like State Historical Commission or State Department of Conservation. Many counties, cities, and towns have such boards or commissions; they may be called Historical Commissions, Landmarks Committees, or the like. In Canada there is *The National Historic Sites Service*, in Ottawa, and similar agencies in the various provinces.

Citizens' Groups

Three distinguished national organizations are active:

The National Trust for Historic Preservation, 748 Jackson Place N.W., Washington, D. C. 20006, was chartered by Congress in 1949 "to preserve for public use America's heritage of historic districts, structures, and objects." The National Trust gives professional advice to groups throughout the nation, holds confer-

ences and seminars, and publishes two magazines, the quarterly *Historic Preservation* and the bimonthly *Preservation News*. Membership is open to both organizations and individuals.

The Society of Architectural Historians, 1700 Walnut Street, Philadelphia, Pennsylvania 19103, is a learned society, founded in 1940. The SAH and its local chapters organize meetings, lectures, and tours. It publishes a scholarly journal four times a year and a newsletter bimonthly. Membership in the society is open to "all who are interested in the study, enjoyment, and preservation of architecture and its related arts."

The Victorian Society in America, The Athenaeum, East Washington Square, Philadelphia, Pennsylvania 19106, was founded in 1966 "to draw attention to the merits of Victorian architecture, design, decoration, and craftsmanship, and to encourage the protection of outstanding examples of the period." The society sponsors meetings and tours, and it publishes a newsletter.

There are thousands of historical societies active in states, provinces, counties, cities, and towns. Many of them are interested in the study and protection of historic neighborhoods and buildings; some have special committees for that purpose. Others are organized to preserve and manage a historic house or local museum. There is also a growing number of groups which salvage architectural relics from buildings about to be demolished. The members of these organizations were once largely older and ultraconservative persons. In recent years there has been a surge of interest in American history and protection of the environment; when you join such a group now, you can expect to meet enthusiastic people of all ages and backgrounds.

SELECTIVE BIBLIOGRAPHY

I have been reading nineteenth-century records for a lifetime; a listing would fill hundreds of pages. I have therefore been forced to limit this bibliography to a selection of twentieth-century books on nineteenth-century American architecture which are accessible to the general reader. For lack of space I have also had to exclude pertinent books on European architecture and also the very large number of relevant articles which have appeared in periodicals. I will be glad to answer inquiries from scholars on specific sources or references. Except for the two works of bibliography, the publication dates given below are those of the *first* edition.

Bibliographies

Hitchcock, Henry-Russell. *American Architectural Books*. Minneapolis: 1962.

Roos, Frank J., Jr. *Bibliography of Early American Architecture*. Urbana, Ill.: 1968.

Architecture, General

Andrews, Wayne. *Architecture, Ambition and Americans*. New York: 1955.

Banham, Reyner. *The Architecture of the Well-Tempered Environment*. Chicago: 1969.

Condit, Carl W. *American Building*. Chicago: 1968.

————. *American Building Art: The Nineteenth Century*. New York: 1960.

Davidson, Marshall B. *The American Heritage History of Notable American Houses*. New York: 1971.

Early, James. *Romanticism and American Architecture*. New York: 1965.

Evans, Walker. *American Photographs*. New York: 1938.

Fitch, James M. *American Building*. Boston: 1948.

————. *Architecture and the Esthetics of Plenty*. New York: 1961.

Garrett, Wendell D., Norton, Paul F., Gowans, Alan, and Butler, Joseph T. *The Arts in America: The Nineteenth Century*. New York: 1969.

Giedion, Sigfried. *Time, Space and Architecture*. Cambridge, Mass.: 1941.

Gillon, Edmund V., Jr. *Early Illustrations and Views of American Architecture*. New York: 1971.

Glassie, Henry. *Pattern in the Material Folk Culture of the Eastern United States*. Philadelphia: 1969.

Gowans, Alan. *Images of American Living*. Philadelphia: 1963.

Hamlin, Talbot F. *Greek Revival Architecture in America*. New York: 1944.

Hitchcock, Henry-Russell. *Architecture: Nineteenth and Twentieth Centuries*. Baltimore: 1953.

Jones, Cranston. *Homes of the American Presidents*. New York: 1962.

Karp, Ben. *Wood Motifs in American Domestic Architecture*. New York: 1966.

Kaufmann, Edgar W., ed. *The Rise of an American Architecture*. New York: 1970.

Kouwenhoven, John A. *Made in America*. Garden City, N. Y.: 1948.

Lancaster, Clay. *Architectural Follies in America*. Rutland, Vt.: 1960.

————. *The Japanese Influence in America*. New York: 1963.

Lynes, Russell. *The Domesticated Americans*. New York: 1963.

————. *The Tastemakers*. New York: 1954.

Maass, John. *The Gingerbread Age*. New York: 1957.

McKenna, H. Dickson. *A House in the City*. New York: 1971.

Moholy-Nagy, Sibyl. *Native Genius in Anonymous Architecture*. New York: 1957.

Morris, Wright. *God's Country and My People.* New York: 1968.

Morrison, Hugh S. *Early American Architecture.* New York: 1952.

Mumford, Lewis. *The Brown Decades.* New York: 1931.

————. *Sticks and Stones.* New York: 1924.

National Register of Historic Places. Washington: 1969.

Pratt, Dorothy and Richard. *A Guide to Early American Homes.* New York: 1956.

Schmidt, Carl F. *The Octagon Fad.* Scottsville, N. Y.: 1960.

————. *The Victorian Era in the United States.* Scottsville, N. Y.: 1971.

Scully, Vincent J., Jr. *The Shingle Style.* New Haven, Conn.: 1955.

Whiffen, Marcus. *American Architecture Since 1780.* Cambridge, Mass.: 1969.

With Heritage So Rich. New York: 1966.

Architecture, Regional and Local

New England

Back Bay Boston. Boston: 1969.

Bunting, Bainbridge. *Houses of Boston's Back Bay.* Cambridge, Mass.: 1967.

Coolidge, John P. *Mill and Mansion.* New York: 1942.

Downing, Antoinette F., and Scully, Vincent J., Jr. *The Architectural Heritage of Newport, Rhode Island.* Cambridge, Mass.: 1952.

Freeman, Donald. *Boston Architecture.* Cambridge, Mass.: 1970.

Hitchcock, Henry-Russell. *Rhode Island Architecture.* Providence, R. I.: 1939.

New Haven Architecture (Historic American Buildings Survey). Washington: 1970.

Randall, A. L. *Newport, A Tour Guide.* Newport, R. I.: 1970.

Rettig, Robert B. *Guide to Cambridge Architecture.* Cambridge, Mass.: 1969.

Survey of Architectural History in Cambridge: East Cambridge. Cambridge, Mass.: 1965.

Survey of Architectural History in Cambridge: Mid Cambridge. Cambridge, Mass.: 1967.

Warner, Sam B., Jr. *Streetcar Suburbs.* Cambridge, Mass.: 1962.

Whitehill, Walter Muir. *Boston: A Topographical History.* Cambridge, Mass.: 1959.

East

Andrews, Wayne. *Architecture in New York.* New York: 1969.

Architecture Worth Saving in Onondaga County, New York. Syracuse. N. Y.: 1964.

Architecture Worth Saving in Pittsford, Elegant Village. Pittsford, N. Y.: 1969.

Burnham, Alan. *New York Landmarks.* Middletown, Conn.: 1963.

Conover, Jewel H. *Nineteenth Century Houses in Western New York.* Albany, N. Y.: 1966.

Detweiler, Willard S., Jr. *Chestnut Hill.* Philadelphia: 1969.

Devlin, Harry. *To Grandfather's House We Go.* New York: 1967.

Dickson, Harold E. *One Hundred Pennsylvania Buildings.* State College, Pa.: 1954.

Foerster, Bernd. *Architecture Worth Saving in Rensselaer County, New York.* Troy, N. Y.: 1965.

Gowans, Alan. *Architecture in New Jersey.* Trenton, N. J.: 1964.

Greiff, Constance M., Gibbon, Mary W., and Menzies, Elizabeth G. C. *Princeton Architecture.* Princeton, N. J.: 1967.

Howland, Richard H., and Spencer, Eleanor P. *The Architecture of Baltimore.* Baltimore: 1953.

Huxtable, Ada Louise. *Classic New York.* New York: 1964.

Jacobsen, Hugh N. *A Guide to the Architecture of Washington, D. C.* New York: 1965.

Kouwenhoven, John A. *The Columbia Historical Portrait of New York.* Garden City, N. Y.: 1953.

Lancaster, Clay. *Old Brooklyn Heights.* Rutland, Vt.: 1961.

Mayer, Grace. *Once Upon a City*. New York: 1958.

Menzies, Elizabeth G. C. *Millstone Valley*. New Brunswick, N. J.: 1969.

Mitchell, Mary. *A Walk in Georgetown*. Barre, Vt.: 1966.

Prokopoff, Stephen S., and Siegfried, Joan C. *The Architecture of Nineteenth-Century Saratoga Springs*. New York: 1970.

Reed, Henry H., Jr. *The Golden City*. New York: 1959.

Rivinus, Marian W., and Biddle, Katherine H. *Lights Along the Delaware*. Philadelphia: 1965.

Silver, Nathan. *Lost New York*. Boston: 1967.

Tatum, George B. *Penn's Great Town*. Philadelphia: 1961.

Van Trump, James and Ziegler, Arthur, Jr. *Landmark Architecture of Allegheny County, Pennsylvania*. Pittsburgh: 1967.

White, Norval, and Wilensky, Eliot. *AIA Guide to New York City*. New York: 1967.

White, Theo. B., ed. *Philadelphia Architecture in the Ninteenth Century*. Philadelphia: 1953.

South

Alexander, Drury B. *Texas Homes of the Nineteenth Century*. Austin, Tex.: 1966.

Barnstone, Howard. *The Galveston That Was*. New York: 1966.

Dulaney, Paul S. *The Architecture of Historic Richmond*. Charlottesville, Va.: 1968.

Feiss, Carl. *Historic Savannah*. Savannah, Ga.: 1968.

Hammond, Ralph. *Ante-Bellum Mansions of Alabama*. New York: 1951.

Lancaster, Clay. *Ante-Bellum Houses of the Bluegrass*. Lexington, Ky.: 1961.

Laughlin, Clarence J. *Ghosts Along the Mississippi*. New York: 1948.

Newcomb, Rexford. *Architecture in Old Kentucky*. Urbana, Ill. 1953.

Nichols, Frederick D. *The Early Architecture of Georgia*. Chapel Hill, N. C.: 1957.

O'Neal. William B. *Architecture in Virginia*. New York: 1968.

Overdyke, W. Darrell. *Louisiana Plantation Houses*. New York: 1965.

Smith, J. Frazer. *White Pillars*. New York: 1941.

Waugh, Elizabeth C. *North Carolina's Capital, Raleigh*. Chapel Hill, N. C.: 1967.

Wilson, Samuel, Jr. *A Guide to the Early Architecture of New Orleans*. New Orleans: n.d.

Wodehouse, Lawrence. *Architecture in North Carolina, 1700–1900*. Raleigh. N. C.: 1968.

Midwest

Andrews, Wayne. *Architecture in Michigan*. Detroit: 1967.

Bach, Ira J. *Chicago on Foot*. Chicago: 1969.

Caldwell, Dorothy J. *Missouri Historical Sites*. Columbia, Mo.: 1963.

Campen, Richard N. *Architecture of the Western Reserve, 1800–1900*. Cleveland: 1971.

Chapman, Edward H. *Cleveland: Village to Metropolis*. Cleveland: 1964.

Drury, John. *Historic Midwest Houses*. Minneapolis: 1947.

———. *Old Chicago Houses*. Chicago: 1941.

———. *Old Illinois Houses*. Springfield, Ill.: 1948.

Ferry, W. Hawkins. *The Buildings of Detroit*. 1968.

Frary, I. T. *Early Homes of Ohio*. Richmond, Va.: 1936.

Kennedy, Roger. *Minnesota Houses*. Minneapolis: 1967.

Keyes, Margaret N. *Nineteenth Century Home Architecture of Iowa City*. Iowa City, Iowa: 1966.

Koeper, Frederick. *Illinois Architecture*. Chicago: 1968.

McCue, George. *The Building Art in St. Louis*. St. Louis: 1964.

McKee, Harley J. *Michigan* (Historic American Buildings Survey). Lansing, Mich.: 1967.

Mayer, Harold M., and Wade, Richard C. *Chicago: Growth of a Metropolis*. Chicago: 1969.

Newcomb, Rexford. *Architecture of the Old Northwest Territory*. Chicago: 1950.

Nineteenth Century Houses in Lawrence, Kansas. Lawrence, Kan.: 1968.

Peat, Wilbur D. *Indiana Homes of the Nineteenth Century*. Indianapolis: 1962.

Perrin, Richard W. E. *The Architecture of Wisconsin*. Madison, Wisc.: 1967.

———. *Milwaukee Landmarks*. Milwaukee: 1968.

Siegel, Arthur. *Chicago's Famous Buildings*. Chicago: 1965.

Torbert, Donald. *A Century of Minnesota Architecture*. Minneapolis: 1968.

Wagner, William J. *Sixty Sketches of Iowa's Past and Present*. Des Moines: 1967.

West

Architecture/Colorado. Denver: 1966.

Baird, Joseph A., Jr. *Time's Wondrous Changes*. San Francisco: 1962.

Carter, William. *Ghost Towns of the West*. Menlo Park, Calif.: 1971.

Dallas, Sandra. *Gaslight and Gingerbread*. Denver: 1965.

Early Cheyenne Houses, 1880–1890. Cheyenne, Wyo.: 1962.

Florin, Lambert. *A Guide to Western Ghost Towns*. Seattle: 1967.

Gebhard, David, and Von Breton, Harriette. *Architecture in California, 1868–1968*. Santa Barbara, Calif.: 1968.

Gebhard, David, and Winter, Robert. *A Guide to Architecture in Southern California*. Los Angeles: 1965.

Goeldner, Paul. *Utah Catalog, Historic American Buildings Survey*. Salt Lake City: 1969.

Kirker, Harold. *California's Architectural Frontier*. San Marino, Calif.: 1960.

Kohl, Edith E. *Denver's Historic Mansions*. Denver: 1957.

Lenggenberger, Werner, and McDonald, Lucille. *Where the Washingtonians Lived*. Seattle: 1969.

Lewis, Oscar. *Here Lived the Californians*. New York: 1957.

McMath, George A., and Vaughan, Thomas. *A Century of Portland Architecture*. Portland, Ore.: 1967.

Marlitt, Richard. *Nineteenth Street*. Portland, Ore.: 1968.

Oklahoma Landmarks. Stillwater, Okla.: 1967.

Old Honolulu. Honolulu: 1969.

Olmsted, Roger, and Watkins, T. H. *Here Today*. San Francisco: 1968.

Steinbrueck, Victor. *Seattle Cityscape*. Olympia, Wash.: 1962.

Canada

Arthur, Eric. *Toronto: No Mean City*. Toronto: 1964.

Blake, Verschoyle B., and Greenhill, Ralph. *Rural Ontario*. Toronto: 1969.

Gowans, Alan. *Building Canada*. New York: 1966.

———. *Looking at Architecture in Canada*. New York: 1959.

MacRae, Marion, and Adamson, Anthony. *The Ancestral Roof*. Toronto: 1963.

Rempel, John I. *Building with Wood*. Toronto: 1967.

Ritchie, Thomas. *Canada Builds*. Toronto: 1967.

Victorian Architecture in Hamilton. Hamilton, Ont.: 1967.

Furnishings and Interiors

The literature on furnishings is enormous, but most of the books deal only with isolated objects rather than with homes. The following are recommended:

Davidson, Marshall B. *The American Heritage Book of American Antiques—From the Civil War to World War I*. New York: 1969.

———. *The American Heritage Book of American Antiques—From the Revolution to the Civil War*. New York: 1968.

Giedion, Sigfried. *Mechanization Takes Command*. New York: 1948.

Lichten, Frances. *Decorative Arts of Victoria's Era*. New York: 1950.

Peterson, Harold C. *Americans at Home*. New York: 1971.

Rogers, Meyric. *American Interior Design*. New York: 1947.

Schaefer, Herwin. *Nineteenth Century Modern*. New York: 1970.

Biographies of Architects and Designers

Baldwin, Charles C. *Stanford White*. New York: 1932.

Fabos, Julius G., Milde, Gordon T., and Weinmayr, V. Michael. *Frederick Law Olmsted, Sr.* Amherst, Mass.: 1968.

Forbes, J. D. *Victorian Architect*. Bloomington, Ind.: 1953.

Gilchrist, Agnes A. *William Strickland*. Philadelphia: 1950.

Hitchcock, Henry-Russell. *The Architecture of H. H. Richardson and His Times*. New York: 1936.

Koch, Robert. *Louis C. Tiffany*. New York: 1964.

Landy, Jacob. *The Architecture of Minard Lafever*. New York: 1970.

Manson, Grant C. *Frank Lloyd Wright to 1910*. New York: 1958.

Moore, Charles. *Daniel H. Burnham*. Boston: 1921.

————. *The Life and Times of Charles Follen McKim*. Boston: 1929.

Morrison, Hugh. *Louis Sullivan*. New York: 1942.

Newton, R. H. *Town & Davis*. New York: 1942.

Upjohn, Everard M. *Richard Upjohn*. New York: 1939.

Zaitzevsky, Cynthia. *The Architecture of William Ralph Emerson*. Cambridge, Mass.: 1969.

PICTURE CREDITS AND SOURCES

The number following each credit refers to the page number on which the picture appears. "HABS" stands for the Historic American Buildings Survey.

Chapter 1

Wood engraving from *Harper's Weekly*, 1869 / xvi

Wood engraving from *Harper's Bazar*, 1869 / 6

Wood engraving published by Redman & Kenny, c. 1879 / 7

Engraving by J. C. Buttre, 1869 / 8

Painting by Alice Barber Stephens from *Harper's Bazar*, 1898 / 9

Photograph by the author / 10

Lithograph from John Riddell, *Architectural Designs for Model Country Residences*, 1864. Collection of Samuel J. Dornsife. / 11

Drawings from *Carpentry & Building*, 1879 / 12

Wood engravings from Thos. E. Hill, *Manual of Social and Business Forms*, 1873 / 15

By Wright Morris, from *God's Country and My People*, 1968. Reproduced by permission of Harper & Row. / 16

By Wright Morris, from *God's Country and My People*, 1968. Reproduced by permission of Harper & Row. / 17

Wood engraving from *Harper's Weekly*, 1883 / 18

Photograph, c. 1905. Philadelphia City Archives. / 19

Engraving from Edward Shaw, *The Modern Architect*, 1855 / 20

Wood engraving from *Scientific American*, 1876 / 21

Wood engraving from *Scientific American*, 1875 / 22

Wood engraving from *Scientific American*, 1876 / 22

Drawing from Julius Hines & Son Mail Order Catalog, Baltimore, Md., 1899 / 23

Stowe-Day Foundation / 24

Painting by Stephen Seymour Thomas, 1884. Collection of Mrs. Summerfield G. Roberts. / 24

Photograph by Cervin Robinson, HABS / 25

Photograph, 1876. Free Library of Philadelphia. / 25

Drawing from *Carpentry & Building*, 1890 / 26

Chapter 2

Engraving from John Britton, *Illustrations of Fonthill Abbey*, London, 1823 / 28

Wood engravings from *The Horticulturist*, 1853 / 32

Drawing by George Platt, undated. Collection of Russell Lynes. / 34

Wood engraving from *The Horticulturist*, 1853 / 35

Photolithograph from A. A. Turner, *Villas on the Hudson*, 1860 / 36

Photolithograph from A. A. Turner, *Villas on the Hudson*, 1860 / 37

Photolithograph from A. A. Turner, *Villas on the Hudson*, 1860 / 67

Plan from A. A. Turner, *Villas on the Hudson*, 1860 / 67

Watercolor, c. 1859. Collection of Richard T. Pratt. / 68

Photograph by Ronald H. Jennings, Virginia Museum of Fine Arts / 68

Photograph by Ronald H. Jennings, Virginia Museum of Fine Arts / 69

Photograph by T. F. Crane, 1860's. Collection of Mary Crane Hone. / 70

Photograph by the author / 71

Photograph by Hans Padelt, HABS / 72

Photograph, 1890's. Collection of Mrs. Albert Frederick Wilson. / 73

Photograph, 1890's. Collection of Mrs. Albert Frederick Wilson. / 73

Three-color wood engraving from a directory of Hartford, Connecticut, 1860's / 74

Photograph, 1866. Collection of Samuel J. Dornsife. / 74

These photographs of c. 1900 were kindly sent to me in about 1960 by a lady in Bryn Mawr, Pennsylvania, who had lived next door to this house as a girl. I regret that I have lost her name. / 75

Photograph, 1866. Office of State History, Albany, New York. / 76

Photograph by William Notman, 1874. Notman Photographic Archives, McCord Museum of McGill University, Montreal. / 77

Photograph by the author / 78

Photograph by the author / 79

Photograph by the author / 80

Photograph by Frances Benjamin Johnson. Library of Congress. / 81

Painting by George A. Frost, 1874. California Historical Society. / 82

Painting by Joseph Lee (cropped), c. 1866. M. H. DeYoung Memorial Museum. / 83

Color lithograph from John Riddell, *Architectural Designs for Model Country Residences*, 1864. Collection of Samuel J. Dornsife. / 84

Steel engraving from *Picturesque America*, 1873 / 85

Photograph by J. Alexander / 86

Lithograph from Warner and Beers, *Atlas of Illinois*, 1876 / 87

Painting by "N.J.," 1865. Lutheran Home for Orphans and Aged at Germantown. / 87

Photograph by the author / 88

Collection of Mrs. James A. Dunlap, Jr. HABS. / 89

Photograph, 1865. Western Reserve Historical Society. / 89

Photograph by E. Richard Levy / 90

Photograph by E. Richard Levy / 91

Photograph by Clay Lancaster / 92

Photograph of painting by Edward Lamson Henry, 1872. Office of State History, Albany, New York / 92

Painting by Eastman Johnson, 1869. Collection of Mrs. John Crosby Brown, II. / 94

Photograph by George Eisenman, HABS / 94

Photograph by Michael F. Penberthy / 95

Photograph by Michael F. Penberthy / 95

Painting by Edwin Romanzo Elmer, 1889. Smith College Museum of Art. / 96

Photograph, 1865. Western Reserve Historical Society. / 97

Photograph, 1891. Dukes County Historical Society. / 97

Chapter 4

Wood engraving from George Williams, *The Holy City*, 1849 / 98

Collection of Mrs. Cyrus P. Bradish / 102

Lithograph from J. D. Scott, *Atlas of Montgomery County*, 1877 /102

Photograph by Arnold Genthe, 1906. HABS. / 103

Photograph by Jack E. Boucher, HABS / 103

Wood engraving from Samuel Sloan, *Homestead Architecture*, 1861 / 104

Plan from Samuel Sloan, *Homestead Architecture*, 1861 / 104

Photograph by William Rapp / 105

Photograph by Cervin Robinson, HABS / 106

Photograph by Cervin Robinson, HABS / 107

Photograph by Frances Benjamin Johnson. Library of Congress. / 108

From *Artistic Houses*, 1883 / 108

Photograph, 1880's. Private collection; courtesy of Heritage Foundation, Deerfield, Massachusetts. / 109

From R. V. Culter, *The Gay Nineties*, 1928 / 109

Chapter 5

Lithograph from Victor Petit, *Maisons de campagne des environs de Paris*, Paris, n.d. / 110

Wood engraving from Edward Strahan, *A Century After*, 1875 / 113

Photograph by Cervin Robinson, HABS / 114

Photograph by Cervin Robinson, HABS / 114

Photograph by Cervin Robinson, HABS / 115

Photograph by Cervin Robinson, HABS / 115

Photograph by the author / 116

Photograph by Jack E. Boucher, HABS / 117

Lithograph from G. B. Croff, *Progressive American Architecture*, 1875 / 118

Photograph by the author / 119

Photograph by William Notman, 1871. Notman Photographic Archives, McCord Museum, McGill University, Montreal. / 120

Photograph by William Notman, 1871. Notman Photographic Archives, McCord Museum, McGill University, Montreal. / 121

Minnesota Historical Society / 122

Photograph by Edward R. Bromley, 1901. Minnesota Historical Society. / 122

Photograph by Cervin Robinson, HABS / 123

Photograph by Cervin Robinson, HABS / 123

Photograph by the author / 124

Photograph by the author / 124

INDEX